SHUT UP AND EAT!

A Journey to a Symphonic Culinary Masterpiece

GIOVANNI SCORZO

Copyright © 2025 by **Giovanni Scorzo**

SHUT UP AND EAT!
A Journey to a Symphonic Culinary Masterpiece

All rights reserved. No part of this publication may be reproduced, distributed, or transmitted in any form or by any means, including photocopying, recording, or other electronic or mechanical methods, without the prior written permission of the publisher, except in the case of brief quotations embodied in critical reviews and certain other noncommercial uses permitted by copyright law.

For permission requests, write to the publisher, addressed "Attention: Permissions Coordinator,"
carol@markvictorhansenlibrary.com

Quantity sales special discounts are available on quantity purchases by corporations, associations, and others. For details, contact the publisher at carol@markvictorhansenlibrary.com

Orders by U.S. trade bookstores and wholesalers.
Email: carol@markvictorhansenlibrary.com

Recipe Copyright: Andreoli Italian Grocer
Recipes Author: Giovanni Scorzo

Creative Contributors - Fred Yager
Book Layout and Cover Design - DBree

Manufactured and printed in the United States of America distributed globally by markvictorhansenlibrary.com

New York | Los Angeles | London | Sydney

ISBN: 979-8-88581-210-8 Hardback
ISBN: 979-8-88581-211-5 Paperback
ISBN: 979-8-88581-212-2 eBook
Library of Congress Control Number: 2025918424

Preface

This is not a book about a chef who "made it." It's a book about someone who refused to become someone else just to survive—and in doing so, he built a life, a restaurant, and a legacy that will last decades. It's also a love story. Between a man and his wife, between a boy and his childhood in Calabria, between a craftsman and his craft.

Let's face it, most restaurants fail. That's not an opinion, it's a fact. The ones that survive? Most of them bend, shift, and morph into whatever they think the public wants. The risotto becomes overcooked rice. The tomato sauce comes already seasoned in the jar. The menus bloat with options. The soul is the first thing to go, sacrificed to keep the lights on. But not Giovanni Scorzo.

From day one, he never compromised. Not once. Not when a food critic gave him hell. Not when a customer demanded extra parmigiano on a dish that shouldn't have any. Not when reviewers said he should "make it more American". Not even when his own business was on the line.

He cooked what he believed in. He served what he grew up with. He treated his food like art, like memory, like family. And somehow, against the odds, without marketing gimmicks and PR dollars, without fake smiles, people came. Then they came back, and then they couldn't stay away.

If you're looking for trends, you won't find them here. No QR-code menus. No Instagram filters. No dishes made to go viral. Instead, you'll find tomato sauce made by hand because it matters. You'll find a restaurant where the chef might come to your table and say, "No, I won't make it that way—but try it like this."

You'll either love this book or hate it. If you hate it, I suggest you read it twice. Because this book, like Giovanni, isn't here to please you. It's here to tell the truth. And truth—like good food—takes time, courage, and fire.

— Marco Santello and Natalie Landman

Table of Contents

Preface by Marco Santello and Natalie Landman vi
Prologue 1
Chapter 1 My Love Affair with Food 5
Chapter 2 Mamma Adele 15
Chapter 3 Mind Bending Food. 37
Chapter 4 Meeting Linda 53
Chapter 5 Coming to America 59
Chapter 6 My First Restaurant 69
Chapter 7 Andreoli, the Taste and Quality of
            Once Upon a Time 103
Chapter 8 The King's Table. 133
Chapter 9 Tell Me What You Eat, I'll Tell
           You Who You Are 139
Chapter 10 My Vision for the Future. 153
Happy Customers and the Dishes That
Make Them Happy. 159
Recipes 194
Chronology 195
About the Author 198

Prologue

What you are about to read is a love story—a romantic adventure about a boy born in a small town in Calabria, Italy, who grows up to become a James Beard-nominated chef and the owner of one of the most beloved restaurants in the American Southwest. I wrote this book not only to share my passionate love of food, or the joy and importance it brings, but also to highlight crucial ingredients that are often overlooked.

I believe if you do something, you damn well better be in love with it. This philosophy is why I can work 16-hour days in my restaurant without complaint. That's when you know it's real love. For me, that love started with my Mamma Adele.

She had a presence that was strong, deep, and grounded, and her love for food ran through everything she did. It wasn't just about cooking. It was about care, respect, and flavor. She didn't just feed us. She taught me what food should mean, and that it was spiritual.

Like most good Italian sons, I worshipped my mamma. But she earned it. She was tireless, generous, sharp-tongued, hilarious, and could cook like a goddess.

From the moment I could walk, I followed her like a shadow, soaking up every scent, every stir of the spoon, every raised eyebrow when something wasn't quite right.

For some people, food is fuel. For me? Food is everything: it's love, language, and life. It's how I show I care. It's how I connect. It's the gift I give back to the people I love. If I sound intense about food, it's because I am. I'm Italian. This is how Italians show their love. I remember being six years old, standing next to my mother in the kitchen while she made meals with incredible attention to every detail. She chose only the best vegetables, the best meat, not to show off, but because love doesn't cut corners.

Those early memories aren't just pictures in my head—they're smells, sounds, and tastes. Those flavors come alive every day at my restaurant, Andreoli Italian Grocer, in Scottsdale, Arizona. I named it after my mother's maiden name because everything I know, everything I make started with what she and all my relatives taught me. Plus, Mamma's family name, Andreoli, comes from the Greek name Andreas, which means manly or brave, a warrior. And, it has a better ring to it than my father's name, Scorzo.

When you eat real Italian food, the kind my mamma made, you feel something. But you have to slow down and take your time to taste it. This is one of the reasons why I wrote this book.

In America, food is rushed. People shovel it in like they're fueling a car. I want to change that. I want to help people remember how to taste again. This book is about how I became the chef I am, and what real Italian food should taste like.

My introduction into the world of cooking started in my mother's kitchen, and by age eleven, I was working in a real restaurant. I did everything that needed to be done from cleaning toilets and scrubbing pots to prepping vegetables, cleaning fresh fish, and making pizza dough. Later, I trained under some of Italy's finest chefs. It was tough. It wasn't like the schools here in the U.S., where you graduate with a certificate and a title like "Executive Chef" after a mere two years, and you can barely make a decent sauce. In the world of cooking I belonged to, we worked, we learned, and we loved.

As I write this book about food, I realize it's really about my life. The two are intimately connected. This book is a map of that life journey, what I call a hallowed culinary path, and I'm inviting you to walk it with me.

If you finish this book and find yourself cooking differently, eating differently—if you stop being just a food consumer and become part of the adventure—then I've done my job. If you can't visit Andreoli, I hope the recipes included throughout the book will bring you the same kind of joy at home.

Writing a book is a lot like making a meal. Both take time, care, ingredients, and a little bit of magic. Both are meant to be savored. And when done right, both leave something behind.

The chapters ahead are filled with stories about food,

family, philosophy, and the people who got me here. Every chapter includes a recipe, often one of our most popular dishes, and each one is part of the story that made me a James Beard finalist.

If you grew up in a multigenerational household, where food was love, and grandma ruled the kitchen, then you already know what I'm talking about. If you didn't? Don't worry. It's never too late to start cooking with care. Never too late to gather the people you love, to sit down, take a bite, and remember what food is supposed to be.

Even if you've never boiled water in your life, there's something here for you. Even if you just read the stories, I hope they make you laugh, make you hungry, and maybe even make you cry. And hey—if you ever find yourself near Scottsdale, Arizona, stop by Andreoli. I'd love to meet you and share a meal.

As for the title of this book, it comes from an old Italian saying I grew up hearing: Mangia e stai zitto. In English? Shut Up and Eat.

So now, I'll shut up. You eat, read, and join me on this culinary journey of life!

— Giovanni Scorzo

CHAPTER 1
My Love Affair with Food

My love affair with food started even before I was born, before I took my first breath. It's a journey that flows with ease and harmony, grateful for God's grace, honoring my beloved parents, family, neighbors, and friends, and carrying forward the Italian culinary traditions that have shaped my life.

This journey started with my cherished mamma, who made sure she only ate and drank the finest foods and beverages to nourish me, the baby growing inside her. She continued with the same care while nursing. I didn't understand it at the time, but her relationship with food became the blueprint of my own. It was a quiet and powerful influence that shaped my entire life.

Born in Calabria, in Southern Italy, I wasn't just another baby entering the world—I arrived surrounded by a large circle of loving relatives, all celebrating my birth with food. I was born into food. I grew up with the Italian palate.

Along with my mamma and papa, there were my nonni (grandparents), my zii (aunts and uncles), my cugini (cousins), and our neighbors. Everyone played a role in shaping my taste, offering meals made with love, simplicity, and tradition. It stirred something deep within me. It was more than eating—it was a transformation. This early immersion in soulful nourishment sparked a metamorphosis that would define my path and reinforce my natural passion for food.

Still, my mamma Adele was the most powerful influence on my relationship with food. Her deep care didn't end with pregnancy—it continued through every meal she cooked. Her kitchen was my first classroom, and through her hands I learned the true meaning of passion, purpose, and love. What she served wasn't just nourishment—it was a daily reminder of who we were, where we came from, and what mattered most. These meals were blessings—gifts from Jesus, expressed through her devotion.

My parents gave us children the best of what they had—love, values, guidance, and, of course, food. And that care wasn't temporary. It's a lasting gift, something that stays with you until the end of your days. Devotion and respect for my parents shaped everything about my upbringing.

That foundation of love and our lifestyle in a small village in southern Italy shaped not only who I was, but how I came to see food. It made what I discovered in America all the more striking.

If you traveled to and ate in Italy, you may already know that the food in most Italian restaurants in America doesn't taste like the food you find in Italy. I grew up in

Italy with strong, unforgettable flavors—certain smells and tastes that are seared into my brain and my stomach.

The difference isn't subtle. To be honest, many so-called Italian dishes served in American restaurants are just bad. They're heavy to digest, drenched in sauce, and lack the freshness, balance, and soul of true Italian cooking. In Italy, food is built on simplicity, seasonality, and spirit. Every ingredient matters. Every dish tells a story. Nothing is drowned or disguised. In many places outside of Italy, however, especially in the U.S. these traditions are often replaced by shortcuts and imitation. Those dishes may look Italian, but they have none of the flavor, none of the essence, and certainly none of the love that comes from a real Italian kitchen.

That's why the food I grew up with left such a deep imprint on me. It wasn't just about taste—it was about integrity. The dishes my mamma and family prepared weren't flashy or complicated. They were made with care, intention, and love. A simple bowl of pasta al pomodoro or a rustic minestrone could bring more comfort than any fancy meal. These were the flavors of my childhood—the ones that shaped my memory, my identity, and ultimately, my own path in the kitchen.

At my restaurant in Scottsdale, Arizona—Andreoli—I try to recreate those same flavors and dishes from my youth. Our tagline says it best: "The taste and quality of once upon a time." This philosophy guides me every day, just as it guided my mother. And as you'll see throughout this book, those flavors taught me how to create—and recreate—the true essence of Italian cooking.

Like my beloved mother, I've become something of a perfectionist in the kitchen. I compare cooking to conducting a symphony orchestra. There might be a hundred instruments playing, but if even one violin is out of tune, the harmony is lost. The sound becomes jarring. You want to cover your ears. That's how I feel when I'm preparing authentic Italian dishes. If even one flavor is off, I start again. Everything must be in balance. Some people say perfectionism is a flaw, but in a chef, I believe it's a strength. Every dish, every sauce, every dressing, all of it has to be just right.

Whether you're a cook, a chef, an electrician, or a mechanic—whatever you do, do it well, or don't do it at all. That's not just a saying to me. It's how I live. I don't cook just to cook—I cook to be the best at what I do. I push myself every day, in the restaurant and at home, to honor the food, the people I'm feeding, and the traditions I come from.

I have to say this plainly: there's a deep cultural divide between how food is valued in Italy and how it's treated in America. In Italy, people ask, "Who makes the best food?" In America, the question is too often, "Who makes the most money?" That difference says everything.

In America, food is often treated like a product, a commodity, something to sell fast and cheap, with little thought for quality, tradition, or soul. I've seen it. I've tasted it and I have rejected it for over 30 years. I've ruined a few anniversary dinners over this. Each time my wife talks me into trying another restaurant and I try to enjoy it to make her happy. However, my brain and stomach revolt when I taste food that I know was thrown together without any real knowledge, or worse, any care of how food flavors blend, or what should be the texture or quality of a dish. How could they serve this? Do they not care? Do they understand that the flavors don't complement each other, and the texture is wrong? I just can't eat it and pretend to like it as that would be lying, and when it comes to food, I don't lie.

For me, food isn't just a job. It's my life. My passion. My everything. It deserves more than respect—it deserves obsession, care, and love. If that makes me a perfectionist, then so be it!

Most restaurants close their doors within a year. The ones that make it longer survive by becoming something they never wanted to be in the first place. They serve whatever they think will sell. The food gets cheaper. The ingredients get uglier. The soul disappears. Somewhere in that sad transformation, the chef loses sight of why they started cooking in the first place. I've watched it and lived it. I've been invited into the kitchens where food is no longer a craft, but a calculation.

From the very beginning, I refused to ever compromise. That might sound arrogant, so allow me to explain. I'm not here to tell you how to run your restaurant. I am not here to tell you that my way is the only way. I am here to tell you that this is the only way I know how to create food. I am also here to tell you what is real for me and what is in my blood. What my mamma taught me, what my nonna fed me, what my hands learned from decades of touching ingredients that still speak to me. Every tomato, every slice of bread, every fish pulled from the sea—they all carry a story. A memory. A moment.

In this book, you'll find a lot of those moments. Some are funny. Some are heartbreaking. Some might piss you off. You'll meet customers who didn't like my food, and I didn't change it for them. You'll hear about critics who tried to put me in a box—and I burned the box. You'll hear about how I built a restaurant that ignored the rules, skipped the trends, and still drew people in, again and again. Why? Because there's something that lives in food when it's made honestly. With passion. Without shortcuts. That something . . . is soul. You can't fake it. You can't buy it, and you sure as hell can't microwave it!

That's why I want this book to be different from just a cookbook. It's why it starts with how passionate I really am with food, from the beginning of my life. Some people say I'm talented in what I do. My answer is, no, I'm in love with and passionate about food. Period!

As I promised, I'm going to end each chapter by showing you how I prepare one of our favorite dishes at Andreoli.

Pasta
Fettuccine, Taglierini, Lasagne, Tagliatelle, Pappardelle

PREP TIME: 10 MINUTES | COOK TIME: 30 - 45 MINUTES
MAKES 4 SERVINGS

INGREDIENTS:

200g Italian 00 flour

100g Italian Semolina flour

3 whole eggs (medium) – room temperature

1 egg yolk – room temperature

1 pinch of salt

METHOD:

Using your hands, make a well shape with the flour. Then put the eggs in the middle of the well with a pinch of salt and beat the eggs with a fork, mixing well. Once the egg is completely mixed, start introducing the flour on the inside of the well, with a fork little by little, until all the flour is incorporated. Make sure all of the flour is mixed in completely with eggs. You should start to see a dough shape start to form.

Continue kneading the dough by hand. Gently bring the dough towards the center (towards yourself), then using the palm of your hand, knead dough the other direction (away from yourself). Continue this movement until a smooth dough ball is formed. (Note: if the dough ball cracks, put a little water on your hands and gently knead for a few more minutes.)

Once the dough has reached the desired consistency, cover the dough with plastic wrap and let it rest for 30 minutes at room temperature.

After 30 minutes, take the dough ball with your hands, and place it on a lightly floured marble surface. Use a rolling pin, starting in the center of the dough, roll the ends towards the center, until you can pass it through the largest setting on your pasta machine. Pass the dough through the widest roller setting, 2 or 3 times. Then reduce to the next setting, and so on until you reach the thinnest setting. The pasta sheets are ready to be cut into your desired shape. Some machines have attachments made to cut Fettuccine, Taglierini, Lasagne, Tagliatelle or Pappardelle.

Cutting by hand: Lightly sprinkle semolina flour over the surface of the pasta sheet to prevent sticking. Starting at one end, fold the sheet inward in 1-inch increments toward the center. Repeat from the opposite end, folding in 1-inch sections until both sides meet in the middle. Using a sharp knife, cut across the folded pasta to your desired noodle width—such as fettuccine, tagliatelle, or pappardelle. Gently shake out the cut pasta and dust with a bit more semolina if needed to prevent clumping.

Chef's Tip: Make sure that you are constantly flipping the dough as you're rolling it out to reach a vertical shape.

Acquolina in bocca! Mouth-watering!

Mamma Adele and me

CHAPTER 2
Mamma Adele

We didn't have running water in the house when I was young. Not until I was about 10 years old. I used to take a bath in a round plastic tub or wash off using the hose outside. My mother would send us to get drinking water. It was about two miles away. You carry two gallons, one and one, because each weighs eight pounds. Five or six of my friends would join me to fetch water for their families. My mother would say, "Boys, when you go there, check for some asparagus." Asparagus grows wild; they are tall, thin, and very tender. When you walked along the path to get water, we would slap our thighs to scare away the vipers in the grass so we didn't get bitten. We'd bring the water and asparagus home, and Mamma would make a frittata.

Without the running water, my mother had to wash the laundry in the nearby stream. She would take the small rug from the kitchen, roll it up, then coil it like a crown on her head, set the basket full of dirty laundry on top, and carry it on her head, her hands free, like the queen of laundry. Mamma was the queen of everything. She ruled with love and passion. Always willing to sacrifice to create our beautiful life. I learned from her that your dreams require sacrifice and dedication. It's a good thing I had those lessons from a young age. I would need them later.

Doing laundry was a major undertaking. It took thirty minutes just to get to the area, and then another ten minutes to go down a steep, narrow alley where it was easy to fall. Then Mamma would reach a small river of fresh spring water called a torrent that came down the mountain. It was so fresh you could drink it. That's where my mother took the clothes to be washed. She would stand there with her feet in the cold water for hours. She did our family's laundry like that until I was about 10 years old, until we moved to the north where she had for the first time a washing machine in the house.

Our eggs were always fresh because we had chickens. When I was nine years old, my mother said to me, "Can you help me with this female chicken?"

"What do you have to do?" I asked.

"She doesn't make any more eggs," said Mamma. "So, I'm going to do surgery."

"Surgery?"

"I need you to hold the chicken still," she said.

I put two bins under one foot, and I held the chicken while my mother took a knife and cut a hole in the chicken's stomach, right through the skin. Then she opened the hole and reached in, felt around, and pulled out her hand. When she opened her hand, there were some stones and pieces of glass.

"That's why she didn't make egg," she said.

Then she cleans the hole with olive oil, disinfectant, and salt and sews it back together. Next day, the chicken is making her eggs again.

My mamma was truly remarkable – her resilience, ingenuity and ability to problem solve, left a lasting imprint on how I have approached the many twists and turns of my life.

Growing up in Italy

I was born in the deep southern region of Calabria, where the land is dry, the people are proud, and the rich history and flavors are carved into stone.

In Calabria, we didn't talk about "farm-to-table." That was just life. Tomatoes came from our backyard. Peppers, onions, potatoes —if you ate them, you grew them, or you didn't eat them. My grandmother would make a meal with only three ingredients and a fire that would taste like a feast.

We were not rich, but we never felt poor, because we had food, not just food for the body, but food for the spirit. The kind of food that came with stories, prayers, and long wooden tables where you had to fight for the last piece of sausage.

My earliest memories of food are not just of taste—they are of heat, smoke, and time. My nonna (grandmother) would cook on a wood-burning stove, outside in the courtyard. No gas. No timers. Just instinct and patience. She didn't use recipes—she used memory.

Her hands knew how much flour was "enough." Her nose could smell when the sauce needed more basil.

As a little boy, I would sit beside her and watch. Not just because I was hungry—though I always was—but because I was in awe. Watching her cook was like watching someone play music by ear. She didn't measure. She felt. She trusted her senses.

Compared to a typical American meal, my childhood felt like a daily celebration of food. We picked peppers and onions straight from our garden, along with vine-ripened tomatoes. If you've ever eaten a tomato fresh off the vine, you know it's a completely different experience from anything grown in a greenhouse. Fresh vegetables were staples in our meals, and everything followed the seasons. Weekly markets were a fanfare of flavor—produce, cheeses, salami. But what I remember most are the scents. You could close your eyes, hold something in your hand, and know exactly what it was—just by its fragrance.

There was always something to celebrate with a feast. Usually, it was for a saint. There were major holidays like Christmas and Easter, but there were also feast days for various saints, the Day of the Dead, and many other observances. In Italy, we never needed a reason beyond tradition and reverence to gather and share a meal. Each celebration came with its own special dishes. It's different in America, where large feasts are fewer and mostly tied to Thanksgiving, Christmas, or Easter. But Italy has thousands of years of history. The U.S., by comparison, is a relatively young country—250 years since the Revolution, or 400 if you count from the Pilgrims arrival.

In Cetraro, the town in Calabria, where I spent my childhood, we had "sagres." These are festivals dedicated to food, saints, and everything in between. The word "sagre" originates from the Latin sacra, meaning holy or sacred.

On July 11, the entire town came alive for the annual feast of San Benedetto, the patron saint of all saints. The streets were lined with families, showing off their homemade salami and "vaiannelli," a type of pepper unique to Calabria—bold, vibrant, and unforgettable, just like the region itself.

A few days later came the feast of the Madonna della Serra, and then Ferragosto on August 15th—Italy's most important holiday. It began under Emperor Augustus as a day of rest after the harvest and was later embraced by the Catholic Church as the Feast of the Assumption of Mary. It also marks the start of summer vacation for all Italians. Coincidentally, it's also my birthday—a fitting day, I'd say. Other major celebrations included the Feast of the Madonna del Pettoruto, one of the grandest in all of Calabria, and the Feast of the Madonna del Carmine, both deeply rooted in tradition and overflowing with flavor. These festivals weren't just occasions; they were declarations of who we are.

In Calabria, they were a vital part of the region's cultural and culinary soul. What began in ancient Roman times as agricultural festivals had evolved into vibrant celebrations, full of parades, dancing, and of course, food. I've attended countless "sagre" over the years, and they never lose their magic.

All of these celebrations shared one thing in common: a love for food. And at the center of every celebration was a meal: sausages grilled over wood, figs pulled from the tree, polenta stirred in a pot as big as a bathtub. These feasts weren't about abundance. They were about tradition. They were about turning what little we had into something transcendent. We didn't need luxury—we had flavor. And flavor, when it's honest, is its own kind of wealth. And let me tell you, we have some of the most extraordinary food in the world. Bold, honest, full of character. Just like me.

That's why, to this day, I refuse to compromise, because I know what food can be when it's respected, when it's made with love, not ego. When food is not about being impressive but about remembering. I wasn't raised with money. I was raised with flavor, and real flavor never goes out of style.

My mind often drifts back to those days. I still see my grandmother in the kitchen, rising early to prepare something fragrant. Every day felt like Easter or Christmas. Homemade meals, fresh ingredients, and simple preparation were the rhythm of life. We didn't call it a Mediterranean diet, but that's exactly what we ate: olive oil, bread, pasta, fish, local seasonal vegetables, and local cheese. Sundays were sacred—always full of family, slow-cooked sauces, handmade pasta, and local wine.

My mother and grandmother were my first teachers, and since we all lived together, I was always by their side.

My grandmother did it all—cleaned the house, chopped wood for the stove, and made every meal. The kitchen was small, so sometimes we cooked outside. Life was simpler, centered around family. Multiple generations lived nearby.

Everything was made from scratch. The tomatoes came from our garden, the fat from our own pig, and the sausage was homemade. Even now, when I try to replicate those dishes, the flavor is nearly impossible to match. We didn't use gas—only wood and charcoal. Sauce simmered in one pot, water boiled for pasta in another, and sometimes something was frying or sautéing in a third.

Today, I replicate those flavors using a brick oven, adjusting the heat with wood, just like they did back then.

Spaghetti al Pomodoro di Nonna Sofia
(Spaghetti with Tomato Sauce)

PREP TIME: 20 MINUTES | COOK TIME: 20 MINUTES
MAKES 4-6 SERVINGS

INGREDIENTS:

2 pounds Italian spaghetti

8 cups Italian Whole Peeled San Marzano Tomatoes - puree*

½ c Imported Italian Parmigiano – grated

4 tbs Extra virgin olive oil

3 ½ tsp salt

1 tbs black pepper

Tomato Puree: Open the canned tomatoes. Using a large bowl and strainer (rest the strainer on top of the bowl, allowing the tomato juice to pour through). Using your hands, break open each tomato, removing the seeds, (tomato seeds are caught by the strainer). Add the remaining tomato pulp to the tomato juice. Throw away tomato seeds. Now with a hand-held mixer or food wand, puree the tomatoes and tomato juice.

METHOD:

Chef recommends preparing/assembling ingredient list before starting to cook.

In a large pot, bring a gallon of water to a full boil.

Add 2 tsp salt to the water.

Meanwhile, use a large iron skillet, over a medium-low heat, add the olive oil, tomato puree and 1 ½ tsp salt. Cook on a medium low heat for 15 minutes, stirring from time to time. Add the black pepper. Continue to cook for 2 to 3 minutes.

Now, it's time to add the pasta to the pot of boiling water. Cook for 8-10 minutes for al-dente. Make sure you stir the pasta while cooking.

As the pasta is cooking, take the cooked tomato sauce and put it in a large bowl. When the pasta is cooked, strain it (save a ½ cup of the pasta water, in case needed later). Add pasta to the bowl. If the sauce seems sticky, you can add a Tablespoon or two of the pasta water, if necessary. Add Parmigiano and mix well. Plate it. Drizzle with extra virgin olive oil.

(Recommendation: Do not add more Parmigiano as a garnish.)

Buon Appetito!

One of my favorite early memories is roasting potatoes under ash. One day, that inspired me to try and create something of my own. I was six years old when I told my grandmother, "I'm going to do something special. I'm going to put a piece of meat inside a potato." I had trapped a little bird using willow branches and Ginestra plants. I cleaned and seasoned it with rosemary, sage, olive oil, and salt. Then I hollowed out a potato and tucked the bird inside. I sealed it and buried it under hot ashes to cook just as I had seen my grandmother do and waited.

When it was done, I proudly served it to her. It was delicious and no flavor had escaped. But my grandmother, being the perfectionist, smiled—and then gave me feedback. "Next time," she said, "less oil. Maybe a little less salt." That was love and my real culinary school.

That was my nonna, exceptional in every way. She even made her own wine. In September, we'd pick grapes and carry them to a cement pool once used to wash clothes. Then, barefoot, my cousins and I would stomp them with laughter while my grandmother watched and smiled. That's how we made wine. Some of my best memories are by the fireplace with her. I'd lay my head on her lap as she roasted sausage or meat for me. She'd tell stories, scratch my back, call me handsome, like my father. Her love and praise helped form the man I am today.

Other times, we picked potatoes. My father and mother planted them high in the mountains, about half an hour from our home. Each seed yielded nine or ten potatoes. My grandmother and I would ride the bus, walk uphill, carrying sandwiches in tea towels—hard-boiled egg and cheese or salami. Then we'd dig with sticks for the potatoes. At five-foot-three, she'd dig up thirty to fifty pounds, and I'd carry them home. It took about five hours every year, and I looked forward to it every time.

The flavor in those potatoes and peppers came from the soil. Calabria's earth is some of the richest in Italy. With such a flavorful product, you don't need spices—just olive oil. I haven't found soil in America that gives food the same taste. Every week, we baked our own bread, enough to feed three families, using a starter that had been passed down through generations. That starter was the bread's soul. My mother, aunt, and grandmother would knead the dough by hand in huge wooden tubs and bake it in a large communal oven, then store it in cloth sacks to keep it fresh. When it was still hot, we used a spago (string) to cut the loaves. We did not use knives. Knives destroy the center of the bread when it's hot.

Some of the loaves were sliced in half and went back into the oven to become crunchy like crackers. Three days later, my friends and I would crawl into the oven to collect the toasted pieces—russicariello. The rest of the bread stayed soft for a week or more, when stored in cloth sacks.

There was nothing wasteful about our food. There was reverence. Even how you ate mattered. I remember being seven, sitting with my grandfather in the late afternoon for a "merenda," a snack. He gave me bread and a thick slice of mortadella, then carefully sliced both and told me, "Eat only where I cut, one bite at a time."

One day, I took a bite before he sliced it.

"Hey!" he said. "You have to slice it first, then eat."

I didn't understand why it mattered. But now I do. I realized that the act of slicing—of showing respect for the food before consuming it—changes how it tastes. It's the difference between shoving something into your mouth and actually tasting it.

The ritual of eating: that's something I've never let go of. In Italy, slicing matters. Hand-sliced prosciutto tastes different. So do bread and cheese. These items, and meat in particular, should be sliced with a knife or a cleaver. Using an electric saw will change the texture and the flavor.

Eating isn't about calories, it's about connection. Every meal is a moment. A pause. A memory. Food is the language we speak when words aren't enough.

In elementary school, I was in charge of the "recreazioni" (morning break and snack time). At 10 am, when the recess bell rang, I'd find a patch of grass, lay out a tablecloth, and set up the food our mothers packed. It was the best part of the day. School was boring to me and my mind was always on what we'd eat tomorrow.

While other kids dreamt about science or music, I dreamt about food. Cooking occupied my thoughts constantly. During adolescence, I continued to learn from neighbors, friends, and elders, gaining knowledge about spices, techniques, and flavors. I paid attention to my palate and stayed true to it. Food didn't just fill me—it stirred my emotions and lifted my spirit. That's why I can't stand badly prepared food. Food still stirs something in me. If it's not right, I won't eat it.

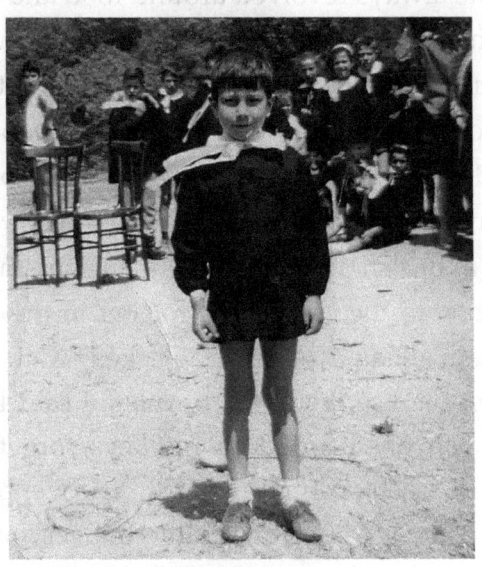

My elementary school days

My love of food kept growing throughout my childhood. I was curious, obsessed even, with flavors and aromas. From early childhood through high school, that obsession never faded. You could call it a lifelong disease—one that will last until I bow before Jesus Christ and thank Him for the gift.

When I was ten, we moved to Liguria, in the northwest of Italy, a region located along Italy's Mediterranean coast and very different from Calabria. My native region, Calabria, was experiencing difficult economic times. Jobs were scarce, and opportunities were even scarcer. That's why my papa moved north to Liguria for work—he found steady employment in bridge construction, and eventually, the rest of us followed. Despite the challenges, there was always a sense of community, resilience, and joy, and my life always revolved around food and cooking.

When we were living in Liguria and I was twelve or thirteen years old, I told my mother I wanted to be a hairdresser. That might sound unrelated to food, but stay with me. I found the best hairdresser in a nearby town—a woman named Lucia, who had worked with Vidal Sassoon, a British hairstylist and businessman. I was the only boy in the salon—the rooster in the henhouse. I made them all laugh. One day, I asked, "Can I cook?"

She let me use their wax burners. I said I needed a car to get fish. She handed me her keys, forgetting I was underage (I was sporting a beard). I drove, bought the fish, and made it along with spaghetti. Everyone loved it.

"We only have one problem," she said. "This place should smell like perfume, not fish. But here's what we'll do—you can cook in my house once a week."

She gave me a key. I cooked for her and her husband, for free, because she was kind. At the salon, I washed hair for money. One customer owned a restaurant, and her hair always smelled like fried oil and fried fish.

Years later, Signora Lucia told me, "That year with you was the best time of my life." I made them laugh. I wore wigs, made jokes, and played the clown. I was just a kid who loved food and women. Even in a hair salon, food had a way of taking center stage.

My salon years

Around the same time, I got my first restaurant job—at The Picnic, a trattoria located next to our home. I was still young, and my parents wanted me nearby. The chef, a kind woman, once offered me a Florentine steak. I couldn't afford it.

"Maybe someday," she said.

And someday came. She cooked it for me and watched as I ate it down to the bone.

"You know how to eat," she said. "I wish I could enjoy food like you."

My parents never pressured me about my future. My mother always said, "Do what you love—but do something." She told me, "If you want to get dirty, work in construction. But if you love food, go to school."

In Italy, after eighth grade, you choose a high school based on your interests—such as geometry, architecture, or in my case, cooking. At fourteen, I entered culinary school. It was mostly fun. I wasn't great yet. The curriculum included languages, math, and law, but I only cared about food. I learned how to move, how to hold a knife, and how to cut.

When I was fifteen or sixteen, I used to go to the beach at night with my friends, hanging out until around midnight or 1AM. There would be 15 to 20 kids, and food would always be in the middle. We would bring the wood and the grill and throw on pork ribs. I was the one who did all the roasting, even though some of the kids were bigger and older, around 18 or 20 years old. I roasted pork ribs or fish. They knew I was the one who would do everything necessary to make a perfect meal. Because of my passion and determination, I can cook anything, pork, fish, and meat. Everything and anywhere.

I liked unusual foods, too. One late-night restaurant served roasted kidney—and I loved it. Roasted kidney is not a normal food for Americans. Some of my favorite foods are not normally eaten here. At Andreoli, some of our specials include kidney, tripe and beef heart. It's delicious!

For example, one of my favorite childhood dishes that most Americans probably haven't heard of is Fava Bean Soup. I have so many fond memories of that soup from home. Just thinking about it makes me emotional. Yet, most people in America don't even know what Fava Beans are. They are these long green beans, a half-inch in diameter and 5-7 inches long. We pull the bean out of the casing, but we keep some of the shells for later to make a pasta dish.

Fava Bean Soup

I love Fava bean soup because it's a refreshing memory of my grandmother and my mother, and there may only be one town that can make this dish – my town. That's because in Italy, even in a span of two miles, the recipe changes, maybe even from one house to another. Recipes change from neighbor to neighbor, who might cook it a little differently.

This Fava bean soup is a poor people's dish, and it is made in a special time of the year, the springtime. When I make this soup, the smells bring my mother back to life, taking me back to my childhood. It's my favorite soup. I think it's my wife's favorite soup too, even though she's a Yankee. We use pig salami; we sauté it with onions and tomato. And we then add the fava beans, followed by the fennel leaves. Not fennel seeds, but fennel leaves, which grow wild in Calabria. The fresh fennel leaves are beautiful. So fresh. I think it's the most important thing ingredient in the soup.

Then we add more onions, a little tomato extract, tomatoes, followed by the sautéed salami mixture. I have everything cut and prepared ahead of time to ensure that all the timing in the dish is right. We have a saying in Italy: the eye of the owner makes the horse fat. It means if the owner is not there, the horse is going to die. Although I work with great people I can trust, especially Rolando Ortega, who is truly from God and has been working with me since he was a teenager. I believe the owner must always be in charge. On top of everything. So, if you're cooking for your family, you are the owner and in charge of making a perfect meal.

Minestra di Fave
(Fava Bean Soup)

PREP TIME: 20 MINUTES | COOK TIME: 20 MINUTES
MAKES 20 SERVINGS

INGREDIENTS:

I use a large pot yielding 20 servings (you can modify by cutting ingredients proportionally)

1 case of long fava beans (You'll need to shell them - 7 lbs. shelled)

You can remove the outer skin from the round Fava beans, but it is not necessary. I keep the skin on. (More fiber, more nutrition.)

1 four-oz can of Italian tomato extract. (puree)

1 Large can of whole Italian tomatoes

Two chopped red onions (medium size)

A cup of extra virgin olive oil, imported from Italy, is best

1 cup chopped fresh fennel leaves.

¼ cup of salt

1 10–12-inch roll of Italian pork salami cut into slices.

6 quarts of preheated hot water

(Optional version – add 4 medium Yukon gold potatoes. Cut into 1-inch cubes, store in cold water until ready to use.)

METHOD:

Put the stove on medium heat.

Pour olive oil into the pan. (Never make the oil too hot or let it smoke, only heat it.)

Sauté the onions in olive oil first.

If the oil gets too hot and you burn the onion, you have to throw it away. It changes the flavor.

Once you throw the onion in, it cools off the whole thing.

Cook for six-to seven minutes, until the onions become golden.

Keep stirring. Don't walk away and do your nails.

After it turns gold, add the salami to the onion and stir.

Add the small can of tomato paste and integrate it into the mixture.

Heat an extra pan of six quarts of water to make it hot so you don't cool off what you have going in the pan already.

Add the large can of Italian tomatoes. Squish them between your fingers as you do to break them apart.

Add a teaspoon of dried hot peppers and stir into the hot mix.

Add the quarter cup of salt.

Make sure your fennel leaves are chopped well.

Add the fennel leaves. This is the most important thing in the soup.

Put your nose over your pan and smell. It should smell wonderful and pungent. Food for me is not supposed to be tasted but smelled. Taste only for salt.

After it's simmered for 20 minutes, we add the pre-heated hot water to the mixture.

Now add the fava beans to the hot water.

After the fava beans have cooked for at least 20-25 minutes and they feel soft when you chew them, you can add the potato, but the potato is optional. If you add the potato before that, it will be mushy by the time the fava beans are done. Add the potato and let it cook for approximately 10 minutes until the potato is cooked, but still firm, not mushy.

My mother made the soup without potatoes, and then other families put the potatoes in. I like it both ways. In Italy, we say the potato is a "swindler" vegetable, because if you cook something good, the potato tastes better than the thing you cook. For example, if you cook a beautiful roast with potatoes, lamb with potatoes, or beef, etc. the potato absorbs the flavor of the roast. It's delicious. That's why we call it the swindler/con artist.

After 10 minutes, you ladle the hot soup into bowls and serve a little bit of Calabrian heaven to your family.

Madonna mia che favola!

CHAPTER 3
Mind Bending Food

I have so many memories of different points in my life where I realized people just didn't get how important food was. How foods they refused to eat will delight their tastebuds when prepared carefully and correctly. Each of these situations make me chuckle. They have two things in common—my desire to change their mind about food and their reaction when I do. I've done it again and again my whole life. I've always wanted people to learn that good food, prepared the right way, is a different experience that can change your life. I love teaching that lesson.

Cooking for the Colonel

When I was growing up, Italy still had mandatory one-year military service for males. When I was 19 years old, I was working in a ski town in Piedmont, and my father called me and said that I've been summoned to the Army. Following one month of basic training I was sent to the base in Florence.

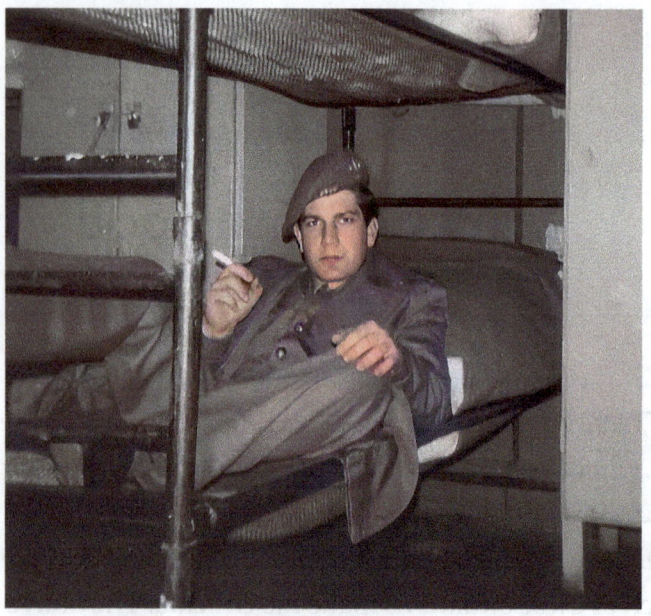

Caporale Maggiore Giovanni Scorzo

When I entered the Army boot camp, I already had a lot of experience as a cook, so they made me the chef for the officers. It wasn't just any kind of army kitchen either. The waiters wore white gloves and dressed like they were serving in the King's palace. I was in charge of the menus. It was a big responsibility, but I liked it.

The officer dining room was set up just like a fine restaurant set up with tablecloths, really pure sterling silver silverware, linen napkins, and crystal glassware. The menu was a full menu from appetizer to desserts, plus a wine list. And every two months we used a have very special dinner for Italian army generals.

One of the dishes is still in my head, It was Arrosto di Vitello with sliced fresh tomatoes and potato puree. Mamma mia che buono!

One day, the colonel, Niccolo Grasso (Lupi di Toscana, Firenze, 78th division) called me into his office. I could tell something was wrong.

"We have a problem," he said.

"What happened?" I asked, standing at attention.

"What's going on with the food?"

"Why? What's wrong with it?" I asked. "Has anybody complained?"

"No," he said. "Everybody's happy."

But I knew something was bothering him. Turns out, it was the money being spent on food. He wanted to know why the food costs were so high.

So, I explained. "This is why we're out seven hundred fifty thousand lire (~$750)—people keep asking me, 'Can you make this?' 'Can you make that?' They let me into the kitchen in the middle of the night—one, two, even three o'clock in the morning—so I could prepare special dishes, like the "milanese". But the ingredients we were given weren't enough to make the food they wanted. So I had to spend more money to do it right."

The colonel stared at me for a long moment, then leaned back in his chair. He wasn't angry—just puzzled.

"So you're telling me we're over budget because the food is too good?" he asked.

"Yes, sir," I said. "The officers are happy because I cook what they actually want to eat—not just what's on the ration list."

He rubbed his chin and let out a deep sigh.

"I've got generals visiting next week," he said.

"They'll be eating here. I want them to be impressed."

I nodded. "Then let me cook what I know. Give me a little more freedom, and I promise they'll talk about the food more than anything else."

He paused again, then smiled. "All right, Scorzo. I'll authorize the extra funds—but you better not disappoint."

"Never, sir."

That week, I went to work like never before. I planned every meal with precision: veal milanese, risotto alla milanese, handmade gnocchi, roasted lamb with rosemary and garlic. I even prepared a tiramisù that made one of the generals put his fork down and say, "This tastes like my nonna made it."

The colonel pulled me aside afterward and said, "They're still talking about the food. One of them wants to bring his wife here next time."

From that time on, I had complete control over the officer's kitchen. I was still a young soldier, but in that kitchen, I was the general.

That experience taught me something important: no matter where you are, no matter who you're cooking for, never compromise the food. Even in the military, especially in the military, good food brings people together, lowers defenses, and raises morale. It becomes more than a meal. It becomes a memory.

Costata di Vitello alla Milanese
(Milanese-style Veal Chop)

PREP TIME: 20 MINUTES | COOK TIME: 10 MINUTES
MAKES 4 SERVINGS

INGREDIENTS:

4 - bone-in Veal Chop, 11 ounces each

5 eggs – room temperature

1 ½ pound clarified butter (you need to make this)

4 cups - Italian breadcrumbs (unseasoned)

Salt and pepper

METHOD:

Chef recommends preparing/assembling ingredient list before starting to cook.

HOW TO MAKE CLARIFIED BUTTER:

Put 1 ½ lb. of butter in a sauté pan, and let it melt on medium heat. Completely melt the butter and let it rest at room temperature for 30 min. When the butter is done resting, take out the foam/top layer of the butter and use the goldish color butter, which will be the medium layer. Set aside the clarified butter that you just made.

*Chef's tip: the bottom layer is the water, and you must make sure not to use that part as it will ruin the clarified butter you have just made.

Tenderize and pound each veal chop until ¼ inch thick.

In a bowl, add eggs and whisk with a fork until they break, do not whip. (Do not add salt to the eggs.)

Place breadcrumbs on a large plate.

Place the veal in the egg mixture, dipping on both sides. Quickly dip in breadcrumbs. Gently tap or press the breadcrumbs onto the veal to help them adhere. Repeat for all veal chops.

In a large sauté pan, add clarified butter (previously made), when it is hot, but not very hot, add one veal chop at a time and cook on each side for 4 minutes. Remove the veal chop and blot with paper towels. Add salt. (Recommend 3 sheets of paper towels for blotting each veal chop.) Ready to serve.

Note: To keep the veal warm until ready to serve, place the breaded cutlets on a baking sheet in a low oven (around 200°F / 95°C).

Rinascere – Be Reborn!

Dinners with Aristide

My customer, Aristide from Italy, would come to Scottsdale, for two weeks straight at a time. He'd come into Andreoli nightly. He'd sit down, sometimes crying, wiping his eyes while he was eating.

"Aristide, what's up?" I asked.

"You are unbelievable," he says. "I'm on vacation every time I am here."

One day, he comes, and the restaurant is full.

"The next time I come here and your restaurant is full, I'm going to bring a bag with cockroaches, and everybody can leave and you can just cook for me," he said.

Then one time he said to my wife, "When are you gonna divorce your husband?"

"Why?" she responded.

"I want to marry him," said Aristide. "I want him to cook only for me."

"If it wasn't for me, you wouldn't have met my husband," said Linda.

Aristide was into my food, always saying, "Make me this, make me that."

The most beautiful part was that he was always by himself. He didn't want anybody. Nobody can sit with him, only me. My food made him happier than anything, and that made me happy.

He'd made a lot of money and retired and told me, "I'm going to open a restaurant and you'll cook only for me in Italy."

"Okay," I said. Then one day, we find out he died.

So sad. We miss Aristide.

Fish That Will Make You Cry

Maurizio Colafranceschi is one of my closest and dearest friends. We met in 1992 and it was a pleasant surprise to meet someone from Calabria. Our friendship was instantaneous. Maurizio had married an American, Kristin, and they had two beautiful girls, Alessandra and Isabella. My wife Linda and I became Alessandra's godparents.

Maurizio worked on and off for me at different restaurants and even helped me drive from Phoenix to San Francisco with restaurant equipment to open Zingari Ristorante. When his wife Kristin came to visit, I made them a special meal. Pesce Spada Calabrese.

Even though Maurizio had my food before, he got overwhelmed. He started crying right there at the table.

"This is so fucking good," said Maurizio, "Memories of my home, near Villa San Giovanni (Calabria), are overwhelming me. You have transported me back in time."

He tells everyone he's been stuck with me ever since. He's stuck with me? I'm stuck with him.

The key to cooking good fish is to start with good quality ingredients. The fish must be very fresh. We have our fish flown in twice a week. Make sure your fish has no smell. If it has a smell, it is not fresh!

When you buy a fish in the store, you need to look at the eyes, the gills to see if they are bloody. And the fish have to be real firm. People can't just learn to cook, they need to understand food. For example, halibut. There are two types of halibut in America. The halibut we use in Italy is very close to the one that comes from the San Francisco coast. It's a similar fish from the sole family. The halibut from Alaska is not for me at all. It's full of mercury. I like the smaller fish, which is about three times thicker than the sole. This fish comes from Monterey, or Tamale Bay, California. That's the one I use.

A few years ago, in my restaurant, I asked a customer who ordered a mixed fish grill plate, "How was the fish?"

"I really don't like it," she said.

"What do you not like about it?"

"It doesn't have any fish taste."

So, I asked, "What do you mean?"

'It doesn't smell like fish," she said.

So, I told her, "Next time you come, give me a call a week before. I'm going to leave the fish outside in the sun for a week. Then I'm sure it will have flavor you will like."

That's why I refuse to eat fish at any restaurant except mine. I know from experience that most of the time it is not fresh. They're a bunch of criminals.

Cooking with Anchovies

If Americans don't know why they don't like something, usually it's because they have never tried it. The perfect balance is artichokes and anchovies. Perfect marriage. Artichokes are sweet, and the anchovies are salty so they balance each other.

So, I asked a customer one day, "Why do you not like anchovies?"

He said, "Because they're too salty."
"Did you ever try them before?"
"No."
I said, "Then how do you know?"
He says, "My friend told me."
And I say, "How old are you?
He said "52."

I said, "What would you do if your friend told you to jump off the Brooklyn Bridge? Your friend told you, but did you try it yourself?"

Then I made the anchovy sauce with the mozzarella for him. But I didn't tell him what the ingredients were.

I asked, "How do you like this?"

"Oh, it's beautiful." He said, "Delicious! Oh, my God. What is it?"

I told him, "Anchovies!"

Anchovies are not all the same. The anchovies they bring into America from Morocco are disgusting. But even the ones from Italy, you have to know how to cook. They are very tasty. If I make you a pasta with anchovy and garlic, you will love it.

Another dish you will love is Dover sole. Here's how I make it:

Sogliola alla Mugnaia
(Filet of Sole with Lemon & Butter)

PREP TIME: 5 MINUTES | COOK TIME: 7 - 8 MINUTES
MAKES 4 SERVINGS

INGREDIENTS:

4 filets of sole (each sole produces 2 filets that are approximately 1/3 lb each.)

1 ½ cups clarified butter

One whole lemon

One bunch Italian parsley

4 Tablespoons of white flour

1 cup butter cut into 1-inch cubes

2 large pinches of sea salt

METHOD:

Clarify the butter first. As the butter melts, it will separate into three layers. The top layer will be foam, spoon off and discard. The next is the golden layer, use a ladle to remove this layer. That is what you'll cook with. The bottom layer will be a bit of water. Throw that out.

Add the clarified butter to a nonstick saucepan.

Take the 4 serving size pieces of cold sole filets out of the refrigerator.

Grate a whole lemon peel. (Try to find thinner skinned lemons to get more juice out of it.)

Cut the lemon in half and get rid of the seeds.

Don't turn the heat on the pan until 11/2 - 2 minutes before you're ready with your fish. The butter should already be warm from clarifying it. You want it to be hot but not burning.

Put some white flour on a platter.

Dredge your fish filets in the flour, coating all surfaces but shaking off excess flour.

Put the filets into the pan in the clarified butter. It should be hot enough to make a slight sizzle but not make any smoke.

Cook for three minutes on each side, two or three minutes each side, until it's a golden color.

Drain most of the butter you just cooked in separate, smaller pan.

Now 6 or 7 take one-inch cubes of fresh butter and put it around the fish in the original pan.

Sprinkle with sea salt generously.

Throw the lemon peels over the top of the filets.

Now the new butter is making the sauce.

Now, squeeze the full halved lemon over the fish through a strainer, while it's still on the flame,

Ladle the butter, lemon peel sauce over the fish as it continues to cook for 2 more minutes.

Roll two more butter cubes in flour and place into pan next to fish, then add a half cup of water.

Inside the fish pan, the sauce will begin to thicken up from the tiny bit of flour, as you continue to ladle it over the fish.

Add another generous pinch of salt over the filets.

Sprinkle chopped parsley over the top of it, as the sauce is reducing down,

Put fish filets on a plate.

Put the sauce back on the flame until it's a little thicker but not super thick.

Pour over the plated filets.

Just perfect. Beautiful.

By doing the sole in this way, there is no breakage in the sauce. Breakage means the oil starts separating from the butter. If you want to make it creamy, you don't have to add cream; you have to just use lemon, then a little water. Then there is no breakage. Breakage is very bad. When you see this at a restaurant, get out of the restaurant as fast as you can!

Impepatina di Cozze alla Ligure
(Italian Peppered Mussels)

PREP TIME: 20 MINUTES | COOK TIME: 15 MINUTES
MAKES 4-6 SERVINGS

INGREDIENTS:

3lbs fresh Mediterranean Black Mussels (scrubbed) –

Purchase tip: only buy unopened mussels. The heavier the weight, the heartier.

6 cloves fresh garlic, remove stamen, cut in half

5 tbs Italian extra virgin olive oil

1 tbs fresh ground black pepper

4 tsp fresh Italian parsley, chopped (from a bunch take the top 3 inches of the bunch to dice to create 4 tsp.

8 oz Italian Pinot Grigio wine

1 tbsp fresh lemon juice

Salt and pepper

METHOD:

Chef recommends preparing/assembling ingredient list before starting to cook.

Giovanni Scorzo

Mussel scrub (cleaning mussels) – Soak mussels in 1teaspoon salt and water for 30 minutes, remove the beard (exterior strings attached to the exterior of the mussel). Strain water.

Place extra virgin olive oil in a large skillet over a medium heat. Add the garlic, and sauté until golden, not brown. Add mussels all at once. Sautee for 7 -8 minutes. Add Pinot Grigio wine. Continue to sauté. The wine needs to completely evaporate, approximately 7 to 8 minutes. Then add black pepper and lemon juice. Cover the skillet with a lid or another pot, continue to cook on a medium low heat. This will allow the mussels to open up.

If there doesn't seem to be enough liquid, you can add ½ cup of hot water, continuing to sautee until the sauce is formed.

Remove lid. Before you serve, discard any unopened mussels. Plate mussels and broth into a soup bowl and garnish with parsley.

Buon Appetito!

Summer I met Linda Rupp, 1985

Linda Rupp

CHAPTER 4
Meeting Linda

In my early 20s, I went to work at the legendary five-star Hotel Savoy in Florence. This hotel dates back to the late 1800s, and it was an excellent place to work, filled with skilled chefs and people who knew how to operate at the highest level. I quickly understood what a competent chef, kitchen, and menu should look like.

In the summer of 1985, I was working at the restaurant Fiorino d'Oro in Piazza Repubblica, in Florence. It was a tourist restaurant, not exactly a place known for authentic Italian food. So why, in God's green earth, would I work there?

Simple. I was 25 and I wanted to meet beautiful women.

The piazza was packed with foot traffic, full of energy, and alive with people from all over the world. I never dreamed that one day I'd meet someone who would change my life forever.

Love doesn't always announce itself. Sometimes it just walks past your restaurant table while you're polishing silverware. That's how it happened for me. I wasn't looking for it. I was waiting tables at Fiorino D'oro when she walked by. An American girl—all curiosity and sunlight, and no clue what she had just stepped into.

Her name was Linda Rupp. She was nineteen and a student at Arizona State University, studying abroad in Italy. She told me she had only been in Firenze for four days, but that didn't stop me. Five minutes after we met, I proposed.

"Will you marry me?" I asked.

"Are you out of your mind?" she responded.

"Yes, I am, but in the best way."

There was something about her. She was smart, grounded, funny, and completely unimpressed by my accent. And she asked me: "Don't you have a girlfriend?" My answer was: "Not anymore".

She thought I was crazy. And I was crazy. I was crazy about her.

She also thought "ciao" was food—like "chow" (she's from Missouri, after all).

Not long after that, on one of my days off from the restaurant, I took Linda to Monte Carlo. We had lunch at a seaside café—a beautiful spot, right where semi-nude bathers like to gather. I was enjoying the view more than she was. Let's just say Linda wasn't exactly thrilled, but she took it in stride.

On another weekend, I took Linda and her friend Nanette on a ten-hour train ride from Florence to Cetraro to meet my mother, father, and sister. There was no room on the train, so we sat on top of my guitar in the corridor, with no air conditioning. It was a long and hot journey. When we arrived, my mother welcomed us with a marvelous meal: homemade ravioli, rabbit, roasted potatoes, and vaiannelli, all served with homemade bread she had baked earlier that morning. By the way, unbeknownst to Linda and Nanette, the rabbit meat they enjoyed happened to be the same rabbit they had petted earlier. When Linda heard about it, she was almost in tears.

After a long, rich, multi-course lunch—about an hour and a half—Linda and Nanette were so full they didn't want to go to the beach. They just wanted to nap. That was Linda's first introduction to my world, but she embraced it immediately and fully. She even offered to help my family with the meal and the dishes, despite her limited Italian. My mother whispered her approval, "You see, she is unlike the other girls you have brought home; this one is a keeper." This reaction was particularly impressive given that previous girlfriends I had brought home were welcomed with my mother blurting out" . . . and who's this puttana you brought home?"

Her summer internship finished in August, and when it was time for her to leave, we said goodbye at the train station. I still remember that teary, heart-wrenching farewell.

I had dated girls before, but Linda wasn't a flirtation —she was a force. The kind of person who makes you realize there's another version of your life just waiting to be lived.

And I wanted that life with her. I had never seen anyone more beautiful than her. She was the perfection of my life.

In the weeks that followed, I spent hundreds of dollars in "gettoni"—Italian phone tokens used for international calls. I was calling America as often as I could. As I mentioned before, when I want something, I don't stop until I get it.

I had never been in so much love in my life. And I wanted that girl. So I did what any young Italian romantic with too much passion and not enough sense would do: I left everything—the Savoy, Italy, my family—and followed her back to America.

Here's one of Linda's favorite recipes from Calabria.

Pitticelli i Milangiani
(Eggplant Fritters)

PREP TIME: 20 MINUTES | COOK TIME: 1 HOUR
MAKES 4 SERVINGS

INGREDIENTS:

4 Japanese eggplant

3 eggs

250 g old bread (remove crust, use only interior), cut into ½ cube pieces

100 g parmigiano (grated)

100 g pecorino (grated)

1 garlic clove (finely chopped)

8 basil leaves (broken into smaller pieces by hand)

Sea Salt

8 to 10 ounces Extra virgin olive oil – to Sauté

1/3 cup plain Italian breadcrumbs – might be needed

METHOD:

Place a medium-sized bowl in the refrigerator – to be used later.

Slice the ends of the Japanese eggplant, do not remove the skin, cut in pieces roughly 3 inches in length. Lay the eggplant chunks in a tray and sprinkle with sea salt, toss eggplant in the tray and let them rest for an hour at room temperature. After an hour, quickly rinse the salt off and blot dry with paper towels.

Fill a large pot with water, bring water to a boil.

Add the chunked eggplant and let them cook completely, approximately 10 minutes on a high heat. Strain the eggplant. After 5 minutes, grab a handful of eggplant and with both hands, squeeze excess water from eggplant. Set aside. Once the eggplant is cool, cut into smaller pieces.

Now, using the refrigerated bowl, place the old bread in water to saturate until the bread is completely wet. One minute is plenty. Now grab the bread and squeeze with both hands the excess water. Set aside.

In a large bowl, combine the bread, eggplant, parmigiano, pecorino, eggs, garlic, and basil. Knead the ingredients by hand well. Take 1/3 cup eggplant mixture and shape into an oval patty, roughly 3 inches long. IF, the dough feels wet (like your patty won't adhere) you can add dry breadcrumbs to the mixture.

In a large non-stick skillet (at least a 12-inch size pan), add extra virgin olive oil, filling to a ½ inch mark. Bring a medium heat. Test the olive oil for readiness, should sizzle when a drop of eggplant mixture is added. Then begin deep frying the patties until golden brown on both sides, 2 - 3 minutes each side. Use a slotted spoon the flip the patties.

Remove, lay on paper towels to absorb excess oil. Sprinkle with grated parmigiano and serve!

Buon Appetito!

CHAPTER 5
Coming to America

By September of 1985, I had a plane ticket to Arizona to see Linda. I arrived in Arizona with no plan, no English, and no idea what I had just done. When I landed at the airport, I thought I was in heaven. But then I stepped out of the airplane door, and I thought the plane was on fire. I thought I was in hell. Welcome to Arizona in September.

Suddenly, I was in the desert, surrounded by drive-thrus, strip malls, and food I didn't recognize. The bread was cold. The tomatoes were flavorless. The kitchens used microwaves. I wanted to cry.

But I didn't. I got to work. I took jobs in restaurants that called themselves Italian but served things like chicken Alfredo, "spaghetti primavera" with heavy cream, and fettuccine alla Michelangelo (imagine if Michelangelo were alive, he would have had a heart attack). I didn't know how to cook any of it. It wasn't Italian food. Not the food I grew up with. Not the food my mamma made. Not the flavors I love so much. The flavors that were stored in my brain. When I thought back about the food in Italy, I was in paradise. Here, I was in food hell.

People say you have to choose between your heart and your stomach. I never believed that. For me, they've always been the same thing.

If I had come to America for fame or money, I would've failed. But I came for love. And love—real love—is stubborn. It doesn't quit when things get hard. It gets louder.

I came to America for one reason – to be with Linda. But for two people to survive in America, I had to do the only thing I knew how to do: cook.

So, between the time I arrived in America and when we opened my first restaurant, I worked in many other restaurants across the U.S. This was all part of my culinary journey, the cities, kitchens, and people who shaped my food philosophy, until I finally brought authentic Italian flavors to an American audience.

One of the first kitchens I worked in after coming to America had a microwave. It sat there like a symbol of everything I didn't understand about this country. They used it for soups, for pasta, and for veal. You'd hear it beep and hum and screech as someone reheated something that was never alive to begin with. No flame. No timing. No heart. Just speed. I didn't come to America to become a line cook for the microwave mafia. But I needed the job.

The restaurant looked like a funeral home—dark, cold, silent. The kind of place where you don't eat so much as wait for food to arrive. I remember trying to explain that I was a real chef. They said, "That's cute. Go wipe tables."

"You speak Italian," the owner said. "The customers will love the accent."

So, because I had an accent and a face that made the ladies smile, they put me in the dining room. I became a curiosity—the "authentic Italian guy." It felt like a performance, and I hated it. It was humiliating, but it paid the rent.

Still, I watched. I watched how Americans ordered. I watched what dishes sold. I watched how the cooks worked in the back, peeling plastic film off containers, pressing buttons instead of turning knobs.

Eventually, I worked my way back into the kitchen—only to find it worse than I imagined. The pasta was precooked. The sauces came from bags. The olive oil tasted like it had been squeezed from old tires. My stomach hurt, but not from eating, from knowing I had more to give.

The menus and the ingredients, they were all wrong. People were asking for Parmesan on everything. They wanted their pasta drowned in sauce. They sent back dishes if they weren't "American enough." It made me sick. But it also made me hungry—hungry to show them something better. Linda stood by me through it all.

Then one day, I was offered a spot in a kitchen run by a Sicilian. The place wasn't fancy, but I saw a gas stove instead of a microwave. I said yes. I created the menu. I brought in everything I knew. I worked long hours, 10am to 10pm, six days a week for months, without taking any time off. The only night I asked off for was Valentine's

Day. I arranged for someone to cover my shift. It should have been simple.

The morning of Valentine's Day, the owner called me and said, "If you don't come in, you're fired."

So, I did what any man in love does: I got dressed. Not for work—for dinner with Linda. I showed up at the restaurant with her on my arm. The owner saw me and looked like he'd swallowed a fork. He didn't even say hello. I walked up to his table, looked him in the eyes, and said, "I quit." We walked out before the appetizers arrived.

That night, I didn't know what would happen next. But I knew I wasn't going back. The lesson was simple: If I had to choose between love and fear, I'd choose love every time.

For the next year or so, I worked in many restaurants from coast to coast.

Linda graduated in 1987, and I wanted to ask her for her mother's approval at her graduation dinner party. That was very scary. I brought 87 roses. That was a lot of money at the time—*eighty-seven roses*!

Linda's mother, brothers and sisters and their husbands and wives, were all there, and I didn't think they really liked me. They thought I was an ET from Italy, coming to steal their daughter and sister, maybe for money or for papers to be an American. My wife says it's not true. That they really liked me.

I told my friend here that to get married, I needed an engagement ring. So, he got me a ring, and I sent the ring to Italy to change the stone. He was supposed to put a diamond in it, and then send it back to me in Arizona. The engagement ring never arrived.

So, here I am waiting to propose in front of her mom and have no ring to propose with. Linda started thinking, I'm not sure about this . . . my family doesn't really know about him, let me graduate and then we'll talk.

But then she said "yes" and told her sister, who lived here at the time, that she was going to get married and we were just going to elope.

Her sister said, "You can't. You have to get married like the rest of us did and give everybody a chance to come." So, we had a wedding in Phoenix. Meanwhile, I had to get paperwork so that I could go abroad because I was considered "out of status" for over-staying my visa.

My dream came TRUE!
Arizona wedding, November 28, 1987

New York

After Linda graduated, she took a job with E.F. Hutton, and part of her training meant she had to go to New York to work at the stock exchange. I didn't want to stay in Arizona without her, so I went to New York with her and got a two-month gig with my buddies helping out at Pappardella Restaurant on 76th Street and Columbus Avenue while she was training at the NYSE.

During my short stint in New York, I became acquainted with the restaurateur, Pino Luongo. Pino was the owner of multiple restaurants in New York City. In 1988, he opened a spot in Long Island called Sapore di Mare (Taste of the Sea), where I took a job. The restaurant was booked before we even opened. It was featured in *GQ* magazine.

In my short time there, I was not the chef. The chef was somebody who didn't know anything about cooking. He was just managing the restaurant. But once I started, they put me in the kitchen. I was very fast. I used to do all the sauté, the veal, the fresh, pasta. I used to do everything; all the pasta was done to order. I liked it there because the food was all original. That's the only restaurant I worked in America, that was good because Pino knew food. He was not a chef, but he had a very good palate, Italian. You know, Italians, sometimes you don't have to be a chef. We know flavors.

While working there I met this beautiful lady, Maria, who wore her hair like a crown. She was maybe 83 years old, Italian from Rome. Her son was one of the top surgeons in New York, and she would come to America to visit him. But while her son was working all day, she said "What am I gonna do?" She wanted to cook. She used to come early in the morning and stay until 5:00 or 6:00 in the afternoon, before going home. She moved like she had flour in her blood and she baked bread the way my grandmother did, kneading by feel, judging the oven's readiness by smell. She made all the vegetables. She made everything. She made every antipasto by hand. Every crostata from scratch. She didn't talk much, but I watched her. Every day. She was the proof I needed that it could still be done. They used to have a beautiful table with her appetizers. She knew how to cook. It helped me forget the bad jobs I'd had in a lot of American Italian restaurants before.

Now I started to envision what a beautiful Italian restaurant could be. There were several things that I tried there that solidified my ideas of what I wanted to do at my own restaurant, and one of them included the display of the antipasto table.

"You love it," she said once, without looking at me. "That's why it'll work."

We weren't partners. We didn't even stay long in that kitchen. But she marked me. Like a whisper I still carry in my ear. Years later, when I opened my own place, I thought of her. And my mother. And my grandfather, who made me cut mortadella the proper way, not bite it like a sandwich.

I also got to see a lot of famous people, like Martin Scorsese, Al Pacino, and Robert DeNiro. The owner used to tell his chefs to let me taste the food before they sent it out to make sure they were good.

I remember Billy Joel came in to eat one day and asked for the Penne Arrabbiata pasta, which is a spicy sauce made with tomato, dry peperoncino, and garlic. So I made it for him, and he sent it back saying he wanted more spice. So I added some more spice and sent it back, and he sent it back to me again for even more spice. So I added a lot of spice, and the owner came back and said, "Now it's too spicy." And I said fuck it. I'm done. I don't want to deal with this guy. You want to make it for him, go ahead.

I also had an encounter with David Letterman. I used to carry perfume samples in my jacket, you know, in those little plastic capsules. Whenever I bent over, the perfume capsules would come out. So, I put them on a shelf over where I was cooking. One night, David Letterman comes in and orders mussels and clams in a light tomato broth. I'm making the mussels and clams, and one of the perfume samples falls into the broth, but I don't see it fall. Usually, I would smell the perfume when you pull at the bottom of the perfume sample, but the sample must not have opened up until after it went to the table because I never smelled anything.

The owner came in the kitchen holding the plastic perfume sample and said, "Whose is this?"

And I said, "I don't know."

"It was in Letterman's dish." He said.

I shrugged and said, "It was me."

Letterman made fun of it when he talked about it on his show, how Gianni Versace perfume got into his mussels and clams, then he said. "They must have a chef in the kitchen with very good taste."

Eventually, I told Pino I needed to open a restaurant in Arizona. He was praying I'd stay. He offered me a lot of money to stay. I said I can't. I needed to go.

He said, Arizona? Why are you going to that cowboy, shit-kicking town? I told him listen, I said, I need to get back to my beautiful bride.

Scottsdale

Linda and I got married on November 28th, 1987. It was a civil ceremony—beautiful and intimate. Then in August the following year, 1988, we were married again in a Catholic church in Italy. Our wedding in Italy wasn't the typical wedding that most Americans are used to. It's an all-day event. We started at 8am, the wedding ceremony at 11am, and we ate and drank until the sun came up. The food never stopped, plate after plate of mouthwatering dishes, celebrating our future and my heritage all in one. When we came back to Arizona, we started putting together our ideas for La Bruschetta.

***

It was 1988, and Linda had a real job—working for E.F. Hutton. She wore suits. She knew about markets and stocks and how to talk to people without yelling. I didn't. But she believed in me. She always did. Even when I said I wanted to open my own restaurant.

"Are you serious?" she asked.

"Yes," I said. "I know what I'm doing."

And I did. Not because I had a business plan or investors. But because I had Linda who was willing to take a leap of faith, and my memories—flavor memories. I remembered every dish my mother made. Every meal my grandmother cooked over a wood fire. Every ingredient. Every proportion.

I couldn't explain it—but it was all in my head. Like a map of taste.

I decided it was time for me to recreate the meat sauce that my mother and grandmother used to make. Mine might not be the same as theirs, flavor-wise, it might taste slightly different, but it would be what I remembered.

CHAPTER 6

My First Restaurant – And the Three That Followed

After two years of working at other people's restaurants, in 1988, we opened our first restaurant, a place called La Bruschetta in Scottsdale, Arizona. Between then and 2007 when we opened Andreoli, we owned or ran five restaurants, three in Arizona, one in Santa Fe, New Mexico, and one in San Francisco, California. Each one was special, with its own stories, its own lessons, and a legacy of honest Italian cooking, built one dish at a time. Each one was a success, and Andreoli is still going strong.

People say behind every great man is a strong woman. In my case, she wasn't behind me—she was standing right next to me, sometimes pulling me forward, sometimes holding everything up when I was falling apart. Her name is Linda. She's my wife, my partner, my anchor.

You think it was just me building these restaurants? Think again.

I may be the one yelling in the kitchen, stirring the sauce, cutting the bread—but Linda was the one figuring out how to pay the bills, how to get the licenses, how to keep the IRS happy, how to raise a family while running a business. We became a team—a great one. We did this for five years before we had kids. We had a lot of fun entertaining people and working together in the restaurant six days a week. Even after we had kids, we would continue working, using a baby monitor so we could hear if they needed us.

Linda gave up everything for this. A stable job. A career path. A predictable life. And for what? To join me in a tiny restaurant with no money, no backup, and no guarantees. She greeted customers when there was no one else to do it. She washed dishes when the staff didn't show. She printed menus on our home computer. She smiled when she wanted to cry.

She let me be me—stubborn, intense, uncompromising—and somehow, she loved me more for it.

People look at the successes now and they think, "Wow, you really made it." No. *We* made it. She made it possible. Without Linda, there is no La Bruschetta, no Andreoli. There is no chef, Giovanni. There's just some guy with an accent yelling about risotto. If I'm the fire, she's the hearth. If I'm the storm, she's the ground beneath it. So go ahead, call me the chef. Call me the artist. Call me whatever you want. But know this: the real power in this story—the one who held it together all along—she doesn't wear a chef's coat. She wears grace.

It all started because Linda believed in me even when I wasn't sure I believed in myself. She worked in finance, so she understood the world of paperwork and profit margins. I understood how to make polenta sing. Together, we figured out how to survive. Eventually, we decided to do what everyone warned us not to: open a restaurant. No investors. No sponsors. Just us. A small space. A simple menu. Food made the way I knew how.

La Bruschetta

La Bruschetta renovated interior

We put everything we had into La Bruschetta, named after an Italian appetizer, nobody in America had even heard of. At every table, instead of a basket of bread, we would serve bruschetta. It was a type of bread topped with chopped tomatoes, basil, and olive oil on top. Scottsdale, Arizona, had never heard of such a thing. I also think that it might have been the first restaurant in America to feature an appetizer table in the dining room, where we would have twelve to fifteen different very healthy vegetables, all on display on a beautiful old vintage table, which now you could not do because everything has to be covered with plastic. The menu consisted of very authentic traditional dishes from Italy.

La Bruschetta started out as a joint venture with my friend, Salvatore and his wife. But that didn't turn out as expected, so we reached a settlement to buy them out, and Linda stepped in to manage the restaurant. At the time, she was still working as a broker at E.F. Hutton, but after the market closed, she'd come straight to the restaurant and work all night. Eventually, we bought out my partner and kept going. It was hard. Linda and I ran the place ourselves. She took over the front of the house and figured out how to run the business side from the ground up.

Although Linda had a background in finance, she wasn't sure how much of that experience could be applied to the business of running a restaurant. Running a restaurant is more demanding than most people realize. We had to undergo design reviews for the building, obtain building permits, and hire contractors to transform the original space from what it had once been into a restaurant. There was the health department, the liquor licenses, training staff, programming the cash register, the printing of menus, and other responsibilities like dealing with wine vendors. Linda had to learn to do all of this.

La Bruschetta was the worst time of my life, nobody understood what I was trying to do – why the pasta is al dente, why is he making it this way, why does the food take so long? Some nights we barely slept. We had babies and bills. I didn't always know how we'd pay the rent. From the moment the doors of La Bruschetta opened, we fought. Not with each other—with the world. We fought against what customers expected. We fought against reviewers who wanted parmesan on seafood. We fought against suppliers who offered us cheap, easy alternatives. We fought because we believed. In the food. In the craft. In each other.

Grand Opening

People kept telling us, "You have to have a grand opening because the people who come to the grand opening will come back." So, we did. We had a grand opening attended by 500 people. We put out this big spread, a 30-foot-long table of food, all free. The people who came loved it. We didn't see a single one come back. That was a shock. The following night after the grand opening, eight people showed up. We were confused and frustrated about why people were not coming. When people did come, they complained that the food was taking too long.

Some nights, we had twenty bucks left in the till. Some nights, we had to choose which bill to pay first. But we always made the food right. Even when no one was looking. Especially then. Because that's the thing about cooking: it's not just about feeding people. It's about feeding who you are.

A kitchen, when it's done right, is a kingdom. Not in the royal sense—not gold or thrones or servants. But in the way that every inch matters. Every tool has its place. Every movement is deliberate. There's a rhythm to it, a kind of heat-borne hierarchy. And if you don't know your role, you burn. That's how I ran all my kitchens. That's how I still do. For me, whoever is in charge in the kitchen is the Executive Chef. Executive Chef means you need to know everything. Hotels name their Executive Chefs, but then there's a pastry chef, and a sous chef, etc. I think you need to know all the stations, or you don't call your chef an Executive Chef. You need to be a master of it all, from bread to pastry to coffee to be worthy of that title.

A kitchen isn't a factory. It's not a performance. It's not a content mill for Instagram. A kitchen is a kingdom, and not everyone is royalty. Only those who respect the product, who understand heat, who know how to listen to the sizzle of onions and the snap of good bread, and who understand that cooking isn't a job—it's a responsibility. That's the difference. You can hire anyone to serve food.

But not everyone can serve the truth.

But back then, at La Bruschetta, we didn't have a kitchen. Not really. We had a room with a stove, a few pans, and a dream. The restaurant was small. The kind of small that makes people say, "This'll never work."

The menu was tiny, but I didn't need twenty-five options. I needed truth. I needed a plate that said, *This is who I am.*

The first few months were brutal. How do we get the word out? We had no marketing, no website, no buzz. Before the internet, you survived on word of mouth—the original algorithm. Some days, we had four customers. Some days, none.

To succeed in the restaurant business, you need customers. We saw that other restaurants had customers. What were they doing? We found out that they had been reaching out to hotel concierges. So, we did too. Linda started visiting the big hotels like the Mountain Shadows, the Hyatt Gainey Ranch, the Phoenician, and the Fairmont Princess. We even invited the concierges to the restaurant and fed them, no charge. They loved it, but then who doesn't love free food? We hoped that if they liked the food, they would recommend us to their guests. The strategy started to work, and eventually, a lot of the guests at our restaurant were out-of-towners or snowbirds. A lot of snowbirds.

Initially, not all of these out-of-towners were good customers. One was so mean to my wife. He had complained about a few things and then said. "I hope by this time next year, this restaurant is bankrupt." So, I told her he can no longer come. So, when he came back, my wife said, "Sorry, but after what you said, we can no longer serve you. So what does he do? He made a reservation under another name and came back anyway. So, I threw him out along with his party. When he gets outside, he says, "I'm going to use all my money to put this place in bankruptcy." Nice guy, huh?

For me, the main problem was that most people didn't understand the kind of food I was cooking. Some did. They were mostly European customers who knew what real Italian food tastes like. They kept me going, my European customers. But most had an Americanized view of Italian food.

Still, it was the food that kept people coming. And eventually, the food kept us going. A friend told a friend. A cousin visited from out of town. A neighbor passed by and saw smoke from the grill. That was our marketing, our PR. Now? It's a scroll. A hashtag. A five-star rating from someone who ate half a plate and didn't like the music. I've never chased publicity. But it found me anyway.

It became a pattern. A new customer would arrive, skeptical. They'd look at the menu and frown. "No chicken alfredo?" No. "No side of spaghetti?" No. "No marinera? Definitely not.

But if they ordered—really ordered—something like the Calamari alla Griglia or Impepate di Cozze or Orecchiette con Broccoli e Salsiccia, they'd pause after the first bite. They'd taste something they weren't expecting, honesty.

Then they'd come back. They'd try something else. They'd ask questions. And by the third visit, they'd look around the room like it was their nonna's house. That's when I knew we had them. Because taste is memory. You don't always know it at first. But once it's triggered—once you remember what food is supposed to be—you can't go back to the fake stuff.

Celebrities

Word spread, and we started to get recognition from celebrities. There was Graham Kerr, The Galloping Gourmet. He wrote about me in his cookbook. Some of the notable people from the Lawrence Welk Show, include the singer, Steve Lawrence, and golfer Gary Player. Then the Formula One people. The most famous, Ayrton Senna, and his girlfriend, the model, Carol Alt.

One of the sponsors of the Formula One race held in Phoenix was Benetton, a clothing company owned by an Italian family, of the same name. An area representative for Benetton, Ettore Nessi, had visited the restaurant, so when Luciano Benetton, the owner of all Benetton companies in Italy and worldwide, arrived from Italy, he also visited the restaurant with my friend, who used to work for him. After that, they came back every night. Phoenix hosted a Formula One race two years in a row, so the second year, they even called from Monte Carlo to tell us he was coming and to reserve a table for four or five nights he was there.

The father of another driver, Alessandro Nannini, was there, and he said something very beautiful. He said, "I need to come to your restaurant, to eat Italian food, the Tuscan food that's better than Toscana."

Giovanni with Ayrton Senna, legendary Formula One Driver

One night, we were closed, and the concierge of the Phoenician Hotel called because a few of the Formula One race car drivers staying there wanted to come for dinner. So, I said, sure, we're open. So the two of us, Linda and I, cooked for them. Then the other drivers found out we were open, and they all came. I remember that instead of three, 50 people showed up for dinner. Flavio Briatore was there. He's very famous in Italy. Also, Ayrton Senna. He only ate pasta pomodoro (tomato, garlic, and basil), he said it made him win.

Critics

Then there were the food critics. I believe that to be a good food critic, you must specialize in one cuisine. You can't have a palate that differentiates various types of cuisine – Italian food is not the same as French, Japanese, etc. Yet, in the US, it seems anyone can be a food critic. Some food critics know nothing about Italian food. But I knew that food critics were important. Reviews could make or break your restaurant.

One day, a food critic named Ellen Jeffords came in. She was a well-known food critic for the Arizona Republic newspaper. At first, she loved our food and our restaurant, and she wrote a positive review that was published in the newspaper. However, when she returned three months later, things turned out quite different. This time, she brought her husband, Mark Curtis, a local TV anchor. He wanted the Bistecca alla Fiorentina (16-ounce T-bone steak). But not the way I make it. He wanted it "more to his taste." He wanted it well done.

I said no.

Not because I didn't care. But because I do care. And when you care about food the way I do, you don't bend it just to make someone feel good. You serve it the way it was meant to be.

A few days later, she wrote another review saying, "The chef's not always right." It wasn't about the food. It was about me. About my "attitude." About my "lack of flexibility."

She didn't critique the steak. She critiqued the fact that I stood by it.

That review could've crushed us. A small restaurant, no big budget, just starting out—we depended on every plate, every customer. But I didn't apologize. I didn't explain.

Because the truth doesn't need permission.

We had the article framed and it's now hanging on the wall of Andreoli, our current restaurant in Scottsdale, AZ. I used to love showing people that article. I'm never going to give you something that's cooked the wrong way. That has always been my practice, and I've never wavered. And at the end of this chapter, I will show you the right way to prepare Bistecca alla Fiorentina.

Another critic came years later. This time, she brought a camera crew and a big smile. She was writing a feature on "authentic Italian dining." She asked if I could make a dish more "viewer-friendly."

"What does that mean?" I asked.

"Less intense," she said. "More… familiar."

Familiar? Familiar is what you grew up with. For me, familiar is polenta cooked in copper pots, ragu simmering for hours, biscotti dipped in sweet wine at the end of a long meal. That's familiar.

What she wanted was something easier to describe in a paragraph.

I told her no. But I still made her a plate. Because even critics, when they sit down and actually eat—really eat—they soften. The food tells them the truth, even if they don't print it.

Then came *Yelp*. And *Google*. And *Trip Advisor*. Everyone became a critic.

You'd serve someone a plate of house-made pappardelle, sauce made from tomatoes picked that morning, slow-braised wild boar, and a grating of pecorino—and they'd give you three stars because "they didn't have ranch dressing."

That's the world now. Instant judgment. Instant gratification.

But I still cook slow.

I still believe in craft. I still believe in listening to the product, not the algorithm. I still believe that a bad review from someone who doesn't understand the food is worth less than a smile from someone who finally gets it.

And those smiles? They come.

People who leave bad reviews—they disappear. People who fall in love with your food bring friends. They bring their children. They come back.

One man came back so often, I started keeping a table just for him. He didn't ask questions. He just sat down and said, "Whatever you're making today—I'll take that."

You think a five-star rating means more to me than that?

The hunger for approval is a trap.

I don't cook for critics.

I don't cook for social media.

I cook for people who are hungry for the truth.

And the truth tastes like this.

La Bruschetta was the beginning, the early seeds, of what became what we do today, at Andreoli. I see it as the first step in our restaurant journey. The second step took us to another state.

Babbo Ganzo

Babbo Ganzo – Santa Fe, New Mexico

There was a developer in Phoenix named Jerry Dick who had built a shopping complex not far from La Bruschetta called The Forum. He was also the building's landlord. This building was where the local Benetton Store was located, and it just so happened that Ettore Nessi, the local Benetton rep, knew this developer and said, "You have to eat at La Bruschetta. So Ettore brought the developer to the restaurant, and he loved it. He was building a shopping center in Santa Fe, New Mexico. He said he wanted a restaurant like La Bruschetta for that new shopping center. He asked me, "Would you consider opening one there, if I gave you a tenant improvement allowance, that would cover everything you would have to do to turn the space into a restaurant?" Linda negotiated a great deal, so we didn't have any out-of-pocket expenses. The work started in 1990, and we opened Babbo Ganzo (which means "cool daddy" in Italian) in 1991.

All this time, we still had La Bruschetta. I had to train a chef to run La Bruschetta so I could go to Santa Fe to open the new restaurant. Guess what? Two months before I opened Babbo Ganzo, that chef, whom I trained, he left La Bruschetta and went back to his old restaurant. So, Linda, she stepped in to run the kitchen in Scottsdale.

As we were making this transition, a family came into La Bruschetta. Their last name was Di Domenico. They said they were from San Francisco but now lived in Santa Fe, so I told them I'm opening the restaurant in Santa Fe. So, they said, "We want to throw you a grand opening party for you."

I said, "Great, because I wasn't going to have one.

And they did! They set everything up and invited all their friends. One of their best friends is Carol Burnett. So, right away, we started attracting the famous people, movie stars, Hollywood types.

Babbo Ganzo was a success from the start. There were more famous people in Santa Fe than in all of Arizona. Besides Carol Burnett, there were Charlton Heston and Brian Dennehy, Jack Palance, Alan Alda, and Val Kilmer. Al Pacino and Ted Danson.

Carol Burnett and me

Brian Dennehy with Mamma Adele and Papa Serafino

Ted Danson, he came into the kitchen one night after eating my food, and he said, "Giovanni, this is the best fucking Italian food I've ever eaten in my life."

The most beautiful thing that happened in this restaurant was when Brian Dennehy called to me and said, "I want to introduce you to a very beautiful lady."

The woman was Ali McGraw. This was very special to me because when I was a little boy in Italy, my sister, who was maybe 14, and I went to see the movie Love Story. I was very sad for like three or four months because the girl in the movie, she died. My sister said, "It's just a movie."

I said, "Yeah, but it's a true story. Why didn't the father, that piece of garbage, give the money to do more tests for the girl? I used to tell myself, "If you forget this movie, then you're a really stupid, no-good person. So, I never forgot the movie. And now she's here, and Brian Dennehy says she's the actress in *Love Story*. And I go, "Wow!"

So, I told her the story, and she hugged me and said, "I'm so sorry."

So, I said, "It's very strange for a boy from a little town in Calabria to come here after twenty years and meet the lady who made me cry and made me sad for four or five months." I thought she was more beautiful when I saw her that day than she was in the movie.

In Santa Fe, there was either the uber-rich, or the Hollywood types. Roger Miller, the singer-songwriter, was a regular customer. He wrote "King of the Road." He used to come over, usually twice a week with his wife. One day Roger Miller's wife came to the restaurant alone.

She said he was really sick. Then, she says: "Can I ask you for something?"

"Sure."

"He has one week to live, and he wants your food. He wants to die with your food."

"What's he like?" I asked.

"The pasta fagioli." So, I made a big portion. Sent her home with it. And that was it. I never saw them again.

People often ask if I learned to cook from my mother. I tell them, "Not really. I saw my mother cooking every day, I saw what she was doing, but I never went next to her and said, "Teach me how to cook." The only time I actually helped my mother cook was when she was visiting us at our Santa Fe restaurant. She made her potato tortelli with parsley for Brian Dennehy. My father and I helped her, which was an absolute joy!

We used to go back and forth between Santa Fe and Scottsdale. I was mostly stationed in Santa Fe and Linda would fly over two days a week to help with the new restaurant.

***

Francesca, our first child, was born in August 1992. Holding her for the first time, I knew my world had changed forever. We decided that one of the restaurants would have to go, so we could be together. The Santa Fe operation was operating well, so we decided to sell La Bruschetta. We continued to commute back and forth between Santa Fe and Scottsdale until La Bruschetta was sold. Linda joined me in Santa Fe with Francesca. Babbo Ganzo was open for lunch and dinner six days a week. One day rolls into the next. Linda became pregnant with our second child, and we started looking for a home to buy. Home prices were out of control. We couldn't afford a $250,000 adobe home with two bedrooms to raise our family. Luckily, we hadn't sold our Scottsdale home, and we decided to put Babbo Ganzo on the market and move back to Scottsdale. Our first son, Gian Paul, arrived in August of 1994. The restaurant was sold shortly thereafter.

Giovanni and Francesca and baby Gian Paul

With some downtime between selling the restaurants, I saw a chance to explore learning more about pastries. I reached out to my friend Romano, and he arranged for an 8-week apprenticeship with a master pastry chef, Cosimo in Riposto Catania, Sicily. It was a wonderful opportunity. Linda was gracious to encourage me to go and away I went. When I returned from Sicily, we began looking for a place to rent to open a new restaurant. But Scottsdale rents had become too high, over $30 a square foot, $5,000 a month (1994). It was too much!

So, Linda got a part-time job, and I stayed home with the children. I loved it. I cooked for them. We'd pop in on Linda at her work. I'd get them bathed and them ready for bed. I did those things and loved it.

I was also baking bread and cakes for local restaurants and selling them. I remember I used to go to the market and sell bread and pastries. I was using our little kitchen, and Francesca, she never liked to sleep alone. So, I had Francesca under my arm while I baked, because as soon I put her down, she would cry. I would pick her up and bake with her all night, under my arm. And then we'd go to the market and sell pastries, cakes, and cookies. No wonder she likes to be in the kitchen so much now that she's grown up.

Roughly a year after we sold Babbo Ganzo, the buyers started to default on their payments. When we sold Babbo Ganzo, we didn't get all the cash up front. It was a structured deal with 25% down and the remainder in installments. They ended up running a poor operation and went out of business, so not only did the monthly installments stop, but now we were on the hook for the rent, which was $10,000 a month. How's that possible? The landlord had us as a secondary guarantee to the lease. We never made that mistake again. The little money from the sale of the business wasn't enough to pay our home mortgage and now the $10,000 monthly rent owed to the Santa Fe landlord.

Just about that time, an old customer from La Bruschetta called us. He asked, "Would we ever want to run a restaurant in San Francisco?" He introduced us to the hotel management at the Donatello hotel, one of the most famous hotels in America.

Their operation was run down, and they were looking for experienced people who could take it over and run it. So, I told Linda, "This is a great opportunity, and I want to tour the property."

She negotiated the lease with. Kawasaki Motors, who owned the Donatello hotel. It turns out, it wasn't just going to be a restaurant we would run. We were going to run the hotel's entire food operation.

Zingari

Zingari Restaurant, San Francisco

In 1995 we opened the restaurant in San Francisco. We called it Zingari which means Gypsies, because after all the moving around we had done, we felt like gypsies.

We ran breakfast, lunch, dinner, a clubhouse on the 15th floor, catering, and room service at the Donatello hotel. But the main focus for me, was the restaurant, and soon Zingari became one of the top restaurants in California.

Linda training Zingari staff

But first, I fired almost everybody. We kept some of the waiters. They used to have a sommelier. They used to have a chef who was sitting in a chair, like American style.

"What are you doing here?" I asked.

"Oh, I'm the chef," he said.

"Are you working?" I asked.

"No, no," he replied, "I control it."

"I don't need people to control it," I said. "I can control myself."

That was his last day.

Then I saw they had been using a lot of ingredients that were garbage. I cleaned everything out. We start with my menu, with my people in the kitchen, that's where I met Rolando, my angel there. Rolando is still with me today at Andreoli.

My wife ran the room service. We had 94 rooms to take care of, in addition to the restaurant, the banquets, and a private club.

So, we're in San Francisco, and we still owed the rent for a closed building in Santa Fe. So, we went to court. We wanted them to allow us to go back in and operate the restaurant ourselves. But the court said no. That denied us access to taking Babbo Ganzo back over, which would have allowed us the opportunity to pay the rent we were being charged. The only thing we had left was the liquor license, which was still in our name. That was worth about $150,000 back then. Our attorney said we would lose everything if you don't sign over your liquor license to them. So that's what we did. And finally, we got that monkey off our back.

After I cleaned house, and get in a new crew, the restaurant is popular again. It's thriving. Busy every night. People used to go for Italian food in San Francisco's Little Italy, but it's garbage. So, they start to come to us. People who wanted real Italian food. Even the other restaurant owners in North Beach used to come to eat in our restaurant. They loved it.

We threw a grand opening, and we got the mayor, Willie Brown, to come. Brian Dennehy and his friend Michael Talbot, who was an actor on Miami Vice, were there. Brian even sent a bagpipe player to perform for the festivities.

Financially, we were doing okay. The restaurant was popular. But we didn't just run a restaurant. As I mentioned, the hotel had a private, members-only club. It had catering, room service, all three meals, breakfast, lunch, and dinner. We did well at dinner or on a catering job, but we lost our shirt on servicing a club that didn't have any members. Didn't matter, we still had to staff it. It was a lot to juggle, especially once we had two kids and one on the way. A year after we got there, Angelino was born in October 1996. Additionally, living in San Francisco was even more expensive than Santa Fe. So, we had to live way out by the San Francisco Zoo and commuted into work. Sometimes, we'd get calls at 4:30 am that someone wasn't going to make her breakfast shift, so Linda would have to cover for them.

Francesca was about to start Kindergarten. We toured the public schools. Not good. Sketchy, Linda called them. That meant private school. But at $3,000 a month, we couldn't afford it.

So, after three years in this beautiful city by the bay, we decided to put Zingari on the market and move back to Scottsdale. It took a while for the restaurant to sell, so Linda moved back to Scottsdale with the three children, and I would commute from San Francisco to Scottsdale on Sundays, bringing tomatoes and cheeses from the Farmer's market with me, and returning back to San Francisco on Tuesdays each week. During that time, I lived in a room at the hotel.

My three angels – Gian Paul, Francesca, and Angelino.

Finally, after being on the market for almost a year, we sold Zingari in 1997, and I joined my family in Scottsdale. We took the money we made from the sale and started to look for a place for our next restaurant from what was available. You never make any money in this business because you sell one, you put all the money into the next one, which costs even more money to build.

Eventually, when she got older, my daughter Francesca would help out. Of all the children, she was the most like me.

One time, I remembered, when we were back in Scottsdale, I was with Francesca, she was about five years old. We were invited for lunch with this family. They were visiting from Missouri. We went to this restaurant, and we ordered. I ordered steak, and Francesca, I don't remember what she ordered. But when they put the food on the table, and she says, "Yuck, this looks disgusting," the people all stared at me.

"I'm not gonna eat this," she said. That's her. Just like me. At five years old. The same. And if she doesn't like somebody, she's done. My wife is more like mellow, American style, but still, she's more strict. She makes me nuts, too, because she likes to argue back. They all do.

When Francesca was old enough to go to school, I cooked lunch for her every day. The school was very close, and I remember I would make pasta for her. She loved it. She was eating better than everybody. Those kids ate their peanut butter and jelly, or bologna sandwiches, each day, wondering why Francesca was so lucky.

LeccaBaffi (Lick Your Mustache)

It's May 1998, and we're back in Scottsdale with another true, authentic Italian restaurant, LeccaBaffi, which means "lick your mustache because the food is so good" in Italian. It featured some of the same dishes we had at La Bruschetta. We were open six nights a week. We served the same simple dishes I grew up with. We only used the freshest vegetables, fruits, imported cheeses, and meat. The seafood was flown in daily.

Like every restaurant we owned, I refused to compromise. Everything, the ingredients, had to be the best.

Linda created a press release that called the food at LeccaBaffi "Italian Regional fare, and Authentic dishes from such regions as Toscana, Umbria, Emilia, Calabria, Lazio, Sicilia, and Liguria." It described the atmosphere as "warm and inviting. The restaurant awakens one's senses with color and food aromas that embark on a Deja' Vu travel to Italy. The lighting reflects this ambiance and highlights focal points within the establishment, such as the antipasto bar and the patron's table, and the glow of the wood-burning pizza oven. Setting off this low-key and flattering atmosphere are cobalt blue accessories, serving pieces and menus designed by Gianni Martino. At the entrance of the restaurant, Chef Scorzo parks his Lambretta (scooter) near his easel, displaying his daily specials."

In 1999, we opened Galileo Bread Emporio, in the same shopping center. This was an upscale bakery and sandwich shop. We used to make everything from scratch. We'd go in at 1am in the morning to make the bread: Ciambella, Filone Toscano, Pagnota Calabrese, and Panini used for the sandwiches. We'd hold back ten loaves for dinner service at LeccaBaffi. In the bakery, we used the bread to make sandwiches. It is the most beautiful bakery. But it was hard running both the bakery and the restaurant.

LeccaBaffi was beautiful, quaint, Linda called it. We did family events, like baptisms, first communions. The kids were growing up. When I wasn't cooking, I was coaching soccer. We lived nearby, so we were happy. We were settled. We started having regular customers. And as we received more five-star reviews, the snowbirds and they're coming back year after year. Other well-known chefs also started coming in. From this, we got more recognition, because all the chefs, the voted for best this or that.

LeccaBaffi received the "Best Authentic Italian Dining Award" from *Phoenix Magazine*, August 2000 and named me "Best Do-It-Yourselfer," August 2001. The Arizona Republic awarded LeccaBaffi the "Best Italian Restaurant" for two consecutive years, September 2000 and September 2001.

Most of our customers were nice, but every now and then, one would piss me off. One day, one of our regular customers comes in with a group of people I don't know, and I take him to a table that's arranged beautifully, nice blue plates, napkins, and a little flower in the middle.

"Is this our table?" he asked.

"Yes, this is for you and your friends."

"There's something missing," he said.

"Missing?" I asked. "What's missing?"

"I don't know," he said, "but the last time I was here, it was different."

I checked over the table closely, to see if there was something missing. There's the salt, pepper, napkins, silverware, these beautiful, gorgeous cobalt side plates my wife loved for the bread, and flowers in the middle.

"There's nothing missing," I said.

"No," he insisted. "Something's missing. The arrangement."

"What's missing?"

"I don't know, I just know it's missing."

So I grabbed this big vase with a giant plant, looked like a small tree.

"Maybe this," I said, and slammed it down on the table. "Here, how about this? You want this tree in the middle of your table? Are you happy now? Or do you want to shut up and eat!"

You know, he was just trying to show off to his stupid friends, but I don't play this game. They eventually sat down and ate. Some people they have this thing with power. When they come and eat, they think they own you. No, they don't own me. They have to do what I say. Now I respect everybody. But when they come in with this attitude, with me, it's a losing battle, because you respect me, I respect you two times more, but you come to in with an attitude, you're going to fly from the restaurant. You need to go.

When you first open, your customers think they know more about your business and they're going to tell you what you should be doing. It happened all the time. Sometimes they would finish something, or three-quarters finish something and then tell you they don't like it hoping that you're going to give it to them for free. Kind of bullying you in a way.

One night these two men and two ladies, were giving us problems. My friend Roberto was a police officer. He used to help with the restaurant. So, I go to this table that was finished eating but refusing to pay their bill.

"They screwed up the order. We won't pay."

"What do you mean?" I asked.

"I'm not gonna pay," he repeated, then added. "I can call the police."

"Hold on," I said, and went to see Roberto to tell him about this customer who is complaining he wants the police. Roberto walks up to the table.

"I'm a Scottsdale police officer, what can I do for you?"

"There was something wrong with the order so we're not going to pay."

"No, you're going to pay right now," said Roberto. "I'm here working, I can see what's happened. You're going to pay."

LeccaBaffi was a place for fine dining, like La Bruschetta was at the beginning. That seems to attract a lot of demanding customers who think you have to do what they say. That's why I changed the Andreoli concept to an Italian grocery with food service. I told my wife I don't want to do ever again fine dining because people treat you like a slave.

Running a restaurant is hard enough without having to deal with bad customers. Then they come in and want you to make something their way. Like they're the expert. No. I will never do that. I'm the expert here. Not you.

One day with LeccaBaffi, the Fire Department, locked our doors, because the bakery had flooded. Why did they do this? Made no sense. Linda had to call a lawyer to make them come back and open LeccaBaffi for the night. It was a mess. The problem with the bakery was that with certain breads, you had to use a certain heat that was higher than usual. But the heat, it made the sprinklers come on, and everything had to go in the garbage. Water was everywhere. But since the bakery was in the back of the building where the restaurant was, the fire department locked everything. This was just an example of the things customers never see.

In 2004, we decided to sell LeccaBaffi. People still didn't really understand the ingredients or what they were experiencing. Like the restaurants before this one, we never compromised. I was the same way with customers at LeccaBaffi as I was at all the others.

We beat the odds. It's like a 95% failure rate to open a restaurant. The fact that we rolled the money over meant each one was a success. But that's what we did, because I didn't want to go and work for someone else. So, we found a way to make it all work.

It would be another two years before we found the spot that would become Andreoli. It was owned by the

Jack in the Box chain, which was looking to sublease it. We signed the lease in 2006, made some tenant improvements, and then opened the doors in February 2007.

As promised, despite what the critics say, here's how to prepare BISTECCA FIORENTINA (the right way)

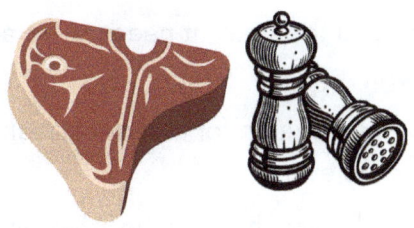

Bistecca Fiorentina
(Florentine Steak)

A good steak begins with the meat itself. Where did it come from? We use only the highest quality grass-fed meats. Since there are only three ingredients, steak, salt and pepper, this recipe is mostly the method I use to cook it.

PREPARATION:

To prepare this dish correctly, you must start with the right cut of beef, which is either a T-bone or Porterhouse steak. I cut my own meat with an ax, a big, heavy cleaver that can chop through any steak bone. But many butchers use electric machines to saw through meat, and those saws burn the meat fiber. This meat is like a woman, soft and tender to touch.

When you go through that bone, you need a sharp, heavy cleaver or ax to cut through it. I cut my steaks about 3 or 4 inches thick. That's what they need to be for a real Bistecca Fiorentina. I know that in Florence they use the Chianina (Tuscan) meat, which is not available in the US. So, I use the same cut of local meat and age it in the same fashion to approximate the original Bistecca Fiorentina.

Before you grill the steak, it needs to be at room temperature.

The next essential item for a perfect steak is a high-quality grill that cooks evenly.

Once the grill is very hot, lay the steak on it. To achieve the best results, ensure the meat comes to room temperature before grilling.

Cooking:

Grill steak it for 7 to 8 minutes.

Once it has cooked on the first side, flip it, and generously add salt and pepper to the other side. Grill that side for 7 to 8 minutes. (If your steak is thinner, adjust the cooking time, otherwise, it will be overcooked.) It's supposed to be rare to medium rare.

Take the steak off the grill and let it rest for a few minutes. Then cut it into slices along the filet side and then the strip side and serve with the bone.

Deliziosa!

CHAPTER 7

Andreoli Italian Grocer, The Taste and Quality of Once Upon a Time

When I opened Andreoli, I knew what I was getting into. Everything I had done before, in La Bruschetta, in Babbo Ganzo, in Zingari, and in LeccaBaffi. It had all evolved into what I was going to do with Andreoli. I called it Andreoli Italian Grocer because it's both a grocery store and a restaurant. You can buy the best Italian food, meats, sauces, and baked goods to take home. Or you can stay and eat in our restaurant. The vision behind Andreoli is to recreate the flavors and tastes my mother and grandmother created when I was a child growing up in Calabria and Liguria. I call it the "taste of once upon a time," because it doesn't even exist in Italy anymore.

When we took over the space, the place was a mess. It was a former Jack in the Box—there was so much work to do. How do you transform a fast-food restaurant building into a home for my cuisine? We boarded up the 'drive-thru' window, got rid of the walk-in freezer and made it a secondary walk-in refrigerator for fresh produce, fresh meats and fresh fish. Cosmetically, we dressed it up—adding shelving for Imported Italian dry goods. Had to demo everything we could to bring life back into the building and open our doors. Along the way, some friends helped out with improvement ideas, Billy in particular. Billy was a long-time friend and LeccaBaffi customer. He was semi-retired cashier at our local supermarket. He was the best promoter of Andreoli in the beginning and an even better friend and customer. He was as proud to dine and eat at Andreoli as we were to serve him.

Billy said, "Giovanni, I know you have a lot of experience, you are the best, but you need to add to the deli cases."

"Billy, they were $6,500 each," I said.

"You're gonna make this money back in less than one year," he said. "People want to see the food."

In Italy we know. The eye, it's bigger than your stomach. So, I listened to him and added the dessert cases, and we started selling a lot of desserts. They wouldn't buy that $5 dessert in the back when they couldn't see it. Once they could look at those desserts, they bought it.

Billy would send everyone who came through his checkout lane our way. At least three or four people a week he sent here. They'd come in and say, "Billy said you are the best. He talks about you like you are a God." Even at Billy's funeral, his daughter said how much he loved Andreoli. People like Billy have been the beating heart of Andreoli.

As business progressed, we decided to renovate the front part of the building—which was desert landscaping—and create an outdoor dining space featuring a wood-brick oven. Linda had to take a full-time job to keep our finances in the black. One day I called her at her work, ranting and raving that the health department was here and not going to let me have the permit to operate the pizza oven. You better get here right now, Linda. I'm gonna kill somebody. I think those were my exact words.

Then the health department came and said, oh, you cannot make the pizza here.

"Why?" I asked.

"Because what about when you take the pizza from here, you open the door, right? You have to go through the entrance to get into part of the restaurant."

"So, what's the problem?"

"What about if a bird poops in the pizza?"

"Guess what?" I said. "I throw it away." Then I added, "What about if a bird poops in the other outdoor patio where people are eating, is it different poop?"

Long story short, we got the permit for the oven, and we started doing pizza two nights a week seasonally. Time flew by and one year became the next. We were blessed to have wonderful clientele and people that truly understood what we were doing and are still doing today at Andreoli's. Then we decided to enclose the pizza patio, make it part of the interior.

That was another big undertaking. When we were under construction, there was a giant sheet of dry wall separating the dining room from the soon to be expansion. I wrote on it for fun, AQUARIUM OPENING SOON.

Customer would often by and ask, "Will Andreoli's Aquarium open soon? What kind of fish are you going to put inside?"

"Well, I'll put calamari, anchovies, lobster, and swordfish," I said. And they believed me. I'm a jokester and a smart-ass, but that is part of Andreoli. The people who love to come here know that!

The Customer is Not Always Right, Period!

I knew the critics might call me stubborn, that some customers would say I was rude, that some people might walk out because I wouldn't put chicken in their lasagna. But I also knew this: The people who stay—the people who come back—they get it. They taste the difference. They feel it in their bones. They don't want to compromise, they want conviction, and I've got plenty of that.

There's a phrase in American restaurants that always made me laugh: "The customer is always right." No, they're not. Sometimes, the customer is confused. Sometimes, the customer is misinformed. And sometimes, let's just be honest—the customer is wrong. I don't say that to be arrogant. I say it to be real.

Because when you walk into my restaurant, I don't want you to just be satisfied. I want you to be transformed. I want your palate to wake up. I want your memory to start working again. And I can't do that if I'm busy bending to every demand that walks through the door.

One time, a woman ordered the carbonara. Real Roman carbonara—made with egg, pecorino, guanciale, black pepper. That's it. No cream. No garlic. No parsley. I brought it to her table, steaming and beautiful, and she looked at me and said: "Can I get some Parmesan on the side?"

"No," I said.

She blinked. "Excuse me?"

"You can't put Parmesan on carbonara," I said. "It's made with pecorino. Different cheese. Stronger. Sharper. That's the flavor you're tasting. Parmesan would ruin it."

She didn't like that. She got offended. She left a bad review. And I slept just fine that night. Because if I start changing what I serve just to make you feel more comfortable, then I'm no longer cooking. I'm performing. And I didn't leave Italy, cross an ocean, open multiple restaurants, and risk everything to be a performer. I came here to feed people what's real.

Here's another one: risotto. Do you know how many times I've been served risotto in America that's just rice floating in cream sauce? That's not risotto. That's wet rice. Real risotto takes time. It requires arborio or carnaroli rice, cooked slowly in broth, stirred constantly, coaxing into its own creamy texture from starch, motion, and patience. You can't rush it. You can't cheat it. You either do it right, or you don't do it at all.

When a customer once asked, "Why is your risotto portion so small?" I smiled and said, "Because it's real."

That's another thing people don't understand, portion does not equal value. You want a mountain of pasta for $9.99? Go to Olive Garden. You want something made with care, from the best ingredients I can find, cooked the way I was taught, by generations before me? That's what I serve.

It's not just about food. It's about truth. It's about integrity. And integrity has no substitute.

Diners, Drive-Ins and Dives (DDD)

Most of the people you see on the Food Channel, they talk garbage. The only person I liked was Julia Childs. Because she was real. No short cuts. I never wanted to be on television. I never cared about becoming famous. I didn't open a restaurant so I could smile into a camera or drizzle sauce with tweezers. I opened it because I had something to say—through food. Not through filters. So, when Diners, Drive-Ins and Dives called, I laughed. I had only seen bits and pieces of the show prior, and the places Guy Fieri visited were nothing like my restaurant. I just didn't think it would be a good fit.

"You've got the wrong guy," I was thinking.

I reached out to my friend, Maurizio. And I said, Mauri, "I don't want to do it."

Maurizio told me, "Giovanni, it's going to be good for you."

So, I took the call to learn more. I had no idea what to expect. It was really nice. This lady just kept asking me questions and you know me by now, I just told it like it was. I told her about all the special things I make at Andreoli, like my homemade prosciutto and my salami.

I asked her if she liked to cook and if she was married. Then I told her if she wanted to make her husband happy, she should make him Bollito and shared the recipe how to make it. Little did I know that she was transcribing our conversation and that Guy Fieri would read it. Guy Fieri said, "A guy that makes his own prosciutto, I want to meet him."

I'll say it. Guy surprised me. He wasn't fake. He wasn't there to 'make me a star'. He actually loved food. Real food. We connected over that. He got what I was doing. He ate what I made and didn't ask me to change a single thing. No fake reactions. No edits to the menu.

He said, 'You do you, Giovanni."

So I did.

We filmed. He ate. He smiled. He said things like "money!" and "that's insane!" and I just kept cooking the way I always had. Guy then asked me, "Are you ready to be part of the Triple D family?" He told us to "be ready because you're going to be super packed."

We had no idea what was coming. Our business blew up! Our customer base grew overnight. We couldn't believe it and I also want to thank Guy for bringing his audience to us—Grazie Mille Guy!

The show aired in February 2019. Since then, business has tripled. Lines are out the door. People flying in from other states. New regulars. Old customers returning. Tourists who had never tasted real Italian food in their lives, now sitting at my table like they had just found religion. It was wild. It was overwhelming. It was a blessing to say the least!

My wife calls it the gift that keeps on giving because it aired again and every time it airs, there's a swell of customers that come in.

COVID 2020

Time continued to fly by, and the world was struck with COVID. Nobody knew what was going on or what to do, and trust me, we were caught in the crossfires. The beginning was the scariest. We were forced to shut our doors. Ironically enough, because our building was a prior fast-food establishment, it had a drive-thru window. This enabled us to offer food for pick up. We threw up an online ordering platform and used our drive-thru window as a pickup window.

During the pandemic, Guy Fieri came up with this creative idea to host a show, DDD Take Out. He graciously invited us to be one of the participants. We packed up and overnighted all the ingredients. It was a contest of sorts; Guy was tasked with cooking the dish from Andreoli and two other restaurants. It was yet another gift from Guy. The television exposure brought attention to Andreoli and helped us out in a tough time.

Our customers were incredible supporters during Covid, too. They bought gift certificates and didn't use them until later. These things kept us alive and our employees afloat during a very difficult time and for that, we can't thank you enough.

The constant change in restaurant regulations—six foot spacing between tables, plastic shields, masks, sanitizing stations—finally subsided.

POST COVID 2021

Celebrities who live or visit Scottsdale, like Alice Cooper, started coming in. Dennis Farina, Gian Carlo Giannini, Evan Longoria, Frank Abagnale Jr., Richard Karn and many, many more.

In April 2022, I was nominated for James Beard Award for Best Chef in the Southwest. I was sitting in my restaurant. It was a Thursday, and a customer came in. He comes in four or five times a week. He says "Congratulations!"

"For what?" I asked.

"You're in the paper."

"I am?"

"For the James Beard Award."

"What's that?" I asked.

And he explained it to me what it is. It's like the Oscars of the cooking world. He opens the paper and shows me the article. It says I was nominated for this award. Here's what the *Scottsdale Progress* wrote: "The awards recognize exceptional talent and achievements in the culinary arts, hospitality, media, and broader food system, as well as a dedicated commitment to racial and gender equality, community, sustainability, and a culture where all can thrive and is considered to be among the nation's most prestigious honors."

We didn't win, but we were still honored and grateful to be nominated. Besides, for me, I win with my food every day because I know it's the best. I don't need an award to tell me that.

Christmas at Andreoli

One of the things customers love is our Christmas Festival. During the season I build a beautiful nativity that has figurines and everything that reminds me of an Italian Christmas. It's over 8-foot long. I wait until Christmas day to add the baby Jesus figurine.

As soon as the nativity is up, I'm in the mood for Christmas. I love Christmas and all that it represents. This time of the year makes me so happy, my heart wishes everyone peace and harmony. It's my favorite holiday.

I miss the food that's connected to Christmas in Italy. So, I decided one day to go all out and present the desserts that are made throughout Italy associated with Christmas. In addition, I offer traditional holiday dishes. I want people to taste the items that are available, so I change up my menu for that. So, we put together a fun, memorable day, and we have a nice turnout.

At the Christmas festival, we add music and entertainment. The people are at tables are talking to each other. It's really a sense of community here. An all-day affair where people socialize. It's one of the things I like to bring from Italy I think you guys are missing in America, socializing with each other. Taking time to enjoy each other.

After seventeen years, people know it's coming and mark it on their calendar. They want to be here. My wife says it's because of me. That Andreoli is more than the walls and the buildout. It's an experience with me as the interactive figure in the dining room.

These days, with Rolando's help and my sons' and

daughter's help, I'm spending more time at the King's table than anywhere else. This way I oversee it all. The King's Table is where I sit with my favorite customers and sometimes entertain with my stories and guitar. There's a whole chapter on the King's Table later, so that's all I'll say about it now.

Now, I want to share some more about Rolando. My wife calls him the angel of the restaurant. He's here every day with me. Rolando and I, we became like father and son. That's why I love him so much. Plus, he grew up with my kids. Look in all these years, he never called in sick unless he's dying. Rolando is not just my backbone. I would call him a real miracle. We couldn't do the things we do without Rolando. He's part of my journey. And I will love him forever.

I get here every day, I kiss Rolando for like two minutes, not in the lips, on the neck. Then I go hug everybody else, and they like it. It's like a family here. At the end of the day, they all give me a hug and a kiss goodbye. I make sure they get home safe.

In America, something I don't like is a lack of respect for workers, maybe because they are not used to a lot of workers. I tell my workers, when they first start, "Come on, guys, you don't look around, you ignore the other workers. This is not your house. When you go to somebody's house, you say 'hi' to people and respect everybody, white, green, pink, black, red, we are all kids of Jesus."

I call everybody in and say, "This is my restaurant, if your family didn't teach you manners, I will teach you, or you cannot work here. You say 'hi' to everybody when you go, even if you don't have a good night." My wife says they are not used to it. I say "tough shit." You get used to it with me. It's my house. If you come into my house, at least that's how I grew up in Italy. For me, respect is everything.

In America, I feel they're missing culture. That's why I'm trying to build this culture of elegance, of respect. I don't want to change America. I would like to help people think about how they enter the situation where they are being served food. Instead of, "I know more than you or, I'm from Chicago." Or, "I know food. I'm from New York. Let me tell you how it's done." It's a kind of disrespect for my position. I'm the owner here, the chef. If you like my food, you're supposed to trust me. I've never been hands-off in my restaurants; I'm totally hands-on even in the kitchen.

Andreoli's isn't the kind of restaurant that turns leftovers into "specials." Too many places in this country do just that, using what they'd otherwise throw away. At Andreoli, our specials come from a sudden memory of Italy, not from excess stock. I don't create them to sell more food or make more money. I create them because I love sharing my passion with others.

I respect my customers, and I respect people, and when I go in the dining room, I want to go with my head up high, not hide. And that's where it is. It's all about love and respect.

Two of my three kids now work in Andreoli.

Francesca and Angelino. When my wife and I get older, I think maybe Angelino or Francesca will take over. Gian Paul, my middle son, his passion is cars, and although he doesn't work at Andreoli, he has a big car show there three times a year. Plus, he worked there when he was a kid.

So, I'm going to let them all say a few words, starting with Francesca, my first born, who is the most like me. She's worked in Andreoli from day one and she's a big part of the place.

Francesca Scorzo

Growing up, I remember always being in the kitchen with my dad. I was daddy's little girl. We're very much the same personality. I have a lot of my mom too, but definitely, more of my dad. We're very much like one and the same person.

I've always loved food. I've always loved cooking. More than being taught by my dad, I've always watched. I think it's something innate. It's like sports. You have it or you don't. You can train and have the best coaches and whatever, but you have to have "it." And, like my dad would say, "it" is in your blood.

I work at Andreoli, and I'm kind of everywhere in the restaurant. In the beginning, it was just me, and I liked it. It was a way to hang out with my dad. I just never left. Now, my main focus is pastries. I'm in the dining room four nights a week, from open to close every day. One of my favorite things is to make the more fun, intricate desserts, like the ones you would see in Europe.

When I worked in Italy, I got to see what a kitchen really is, and those kitchens run very much like my dad runs his. You have to have thick skin to work in a restaurant. You also need have to have a very strong personality, especially if you work in the kitchen. It's a tough place to be.

It's like being a teacher. Teachers are the most underpaid, undervalued people in the world. They are with your kids nine hours a day. They tutor them after school. They get there before the kids, and they do so much prep work. I got my master's in teaching, so I really got into that whole teaching realm. They don't get as much credit as they should. I think the same thing goes for the restaurant industry. No one can appreciate what it takes to run a great restaurant that produces exceptional food until you've been in the trenches and done it.

For example, we close at nine, but there are people who come in at 8:55 and expect you to cook for them, and they'll sit there until 10:30 like they don't care. You're there to serve them. The hospitality industry is a place where you really have to love what you do; you really have to want to be there. Same with restaurants. You really have to love it. You don't go into it for the money. Or because maybe one day you'll be like Guy Fieri. You go into it because you love what you do. My dad loves what he does, and it shows through his food. And through his personality.

My father imports most of our food. He'll be up on the phone at two o'clock in the morning ordering fish. He's all about quality. He wants the best of everything.

He never takes the easy way. Everything we have is grass-fed, organic, prime, fresh, and overnighted. In my opinion, my dad is not valued the way he should be. My father is very passionate in everything he does. As a father, as a chef.

His family is everything. At Andreoli, my dad treats everyone like family, especially the people who work here. Like, Rolando. He's been with my dad for thirty years, since I was two. He's like an older brother. He has three daughters and a little boy, they're like my nieces and nephew, and my father feels like a grandfather to those kids.

Rolando is Dad's right-hand man. He does everything. He started when he was fourteen. Now he's forty-two. He's there every morning. He opens up the restaurant. When we're closed, he's there. When we're out of town, he's there. He works in the back and the front as well. He's like the second boss to my dad.

My dad is very prideful in his work. He's successful now, but it took a long time and his stubborn uncompromising personality to get there. It wasn't just all given to him. It wasn't like I knew this person, and they were able to get me on that show. It was all my dad's hard work, and my mom as well. He couldn't do it without my mom. But what they've done and where they are today is because of how much work and love and passion they put into it, not because they had connections or paid someone. We've never paid for marketing or sponsored ads. My dad has been asked to be on multiple TV shows, but he doesn't go on because he doesn't agree with what they stand for or what they do.

If there's one thing that embodies Andreoli more than anything else, it's the King's Table. Andreoli's wouldn't be the same without it. It's my dad's special table, and it's where he sits with his friends, his posse, and anyone he invites to sit there. Only certain people can sit there. If you're at the table, you're the cool kid.

He loves to be the center of attention. He loves to tell stories and bring people together, and that table does that. Sometimes, my dad will take out his guitar and start playing and singing, in the middle of lunch.

It's annoying because you can't hear the customers to take their order. But he doesn't care, and the customers love it. They'll sing along and take his picture. It's not like a normal restaurant environment, but people think it's really cool. The table embodies who my dad is.

At Andreoli, my dad's food is better than you get in Italy. It brings you back to a place . . . it tastes good. His palate is his brain.

(Read more about The King's Table in Chapter 8)

Next up is my middle son, Gian Paul, who shares my passions for cars and soccer, but decided working in a restaurant is not what he loves the most, which is cars.

Gian Paul Scorzo

I'm the middle child, the black sheep of the family, the only one who doesn't work at the restaurant. My passion is cars, and my business is selling expensive cars. I'm successful because I love and enjoy what I do, just like my dad.

I'm like my dad in a couple of other ways, too. I got my passion for cars from my dad. He's always been an Italian car guy. We'd wake up in the morning and watch Formula One together. I grew up watching cars with him. My first toys were always cars. I just took the little toy Hot Wheels and made that my life.

When I was a kid, I was something of a troublemaker, just like my dad when he was young. I would get suspended from school, and my parents would make me wait tables at the restaurant to work on my "people" skills. When I was fifteen, for punishment, they made me get up at 4:30 in the morning to make bread before I went to high school. I hated it because I always stayed up late. So, I'd try to get out of making the bread by asking my dad's right-hand man, Rolando, who was there every morning, to make the bread. I'd go to sleep in the office and pretend like I did it. Rolando covered for me until my dad caught on, and I had to grow up and take responsibility. It was cool that my dad was teaching me the recipe of his coveted bread. It's one of the most famous things he makes, with starter yeast over 30 years old, and so popular with our customers. It was one of my most memorable experiences.

As I got older, I'd pick up a couple of shifts at the restaurant to earn a little extra cash and after college, I worked in the kitchen for about a year, until I decided it was time to take my own path. I love the restaurant, and I love the food, but I wanted to earn money my own way. I worked for Morgan Stanley for a while, but I really wanted to follow my passion for cars. When I was fifteen or sixteen, I apprenticed for a mechanic who specialized in vintage Ferraris, which is primarily what I sell now. I learned how to work on cars, and throughout that time, I transitioned into selling them. Sotheby's acquired part of my business, so now I work with them.

Even though I don't work at Andreoli's, there's a connection through my car business. I hold events there three times a year, called Expressos and Engines, where clients show off their beautiful, expensive cars. They fill up the parking lots with over 200 supercars from Ferraris and Porsches to McLarens and Lamborghinis. My brother and sister make the croissants and coffee, and I get out there and network and socialize. My dad is happy that I'm doing something I love and knows the shows at the restaurant are good for my business as well as his.

Another big part of our life was soccer. My dad coached me and my brother for five years. Soccer was and is a huge passion for us. It even ties into the restaurant because we watch games there. Italian fans come in, and we decorate it with all the flags. If there's a game day and there's an Italian team playing, you're not going to find a seat. One day an Italian team was playing Barcelona and the Italian team won, so my dad grabbed a bottle of champagne, shook it up, and started spraying it all over his friends. Everybody was laughing and having a good time.

The biggest thing about Andreoli is its authenticity and its atmosphere. Other Italian restaurants are manipulated, and their food is Americanized to be like what people want. Andreoli is the epitome of authenticity, even down to the tables and chairs. Nothing matches. It's all antique furniture and shelving that we bring in from Italy.

Andreoli is also a homey place. You come in, you see our soccer trophies on the wall, the family pictures, and it's just a very good atmosphere inside. You come in, you see the Italian guys yelling at each other, arguing. You see the antique furniture, the soccer game on the TV, the old Alfa Romeo parked outside the front, or the Ferrari. And you're like, ok, I'm in the right spot.

The food just speaks for itself. Even the Italians who own other Italian restaurants in the area eat at my dad's restaurant every day. The food at Andreoli is made from real Italian recipes that don't over complicate things with so many different kinds of ingredients. Italian food is simple. You eat some amazing food, get a little taste of Italy, a real, authentic experience.

There's a mentality I got from my parents, especially from my dad, from running his business, and my mom as well. Don't cut any corners. My dad doesn't cut a single corner with food. With the quality of the products he brings in, he's very consistent about that.

My dad is the mad genius, and my mom is the one who binds it all together and makes sure it doesn't fall apart. My brother is learning the business. He's there in the morning to make the bread. He makes the dough, the croissants, and the sauces. He knows how to run or manage the restaurant. He sets the schedules for the employees, and he does a lot of the stuff my dad didn't do. He's on the right trajectory to be a successful restaurateur.

For me, I'm trying to do the same thing with cars and using my creative side to grow the business. I learned that by watching my dad cook food and seeing the passion that comes through it. I just want to say that Italian food is all about passion, and my dad has figured out a way to take his passion and creativity and put it on a plate and make it something that can be enjoyed by everybody.

Now, you'll hear from my youngest son, Angelino, who is learning everything there is to know about running a restaurant. That's so I don't worry if one day Linda and I decide we're too old to do it. He'll be ready.

Angelino Scorzo

I started working at Andreoli during my senior year of college. I loved it. I loved the food and I loved the people, and making connections. We have amazing customers. It feels like home; it doesn't feel like work. When it gets really busy, it's not as much fun but I love it when we can put a smile on people's faces, when I see them enjoying the food my father created, there's nothing better than that.

When I was younger, my dream was to be a professional soccer player. I played soccer all through high school and college. I got my athletic ability from my mother and my cooking ability from my father.

After high school, I wanted to go to Germany to play soccer, but I got an academic scholarship to Arizona State University (ASU), and my mother made me go. It did pay for my schooling. I did the online program, but even then, I had to attend two classes on campus during my first semester of my freshman year and the last semester of my senior year. The rest was online and that allowed me to travel back and forth between soccer trials and clubs.

Then, during my sophomore year, I suffered this gnarly concussion playing soccer. The game before I had been kneed in the face and was partially blind for two weeks. Suddenly, I didn't know if I wanted to keep going down this route. I asked myself, "Do I really want to do this for the rest of my life?" I don't know if soccer is worth my eyesight.

Senior year, I majored in finance and interned at a Real Estate Investment Trust. They dealt with different kinds of businesses, so I was able to see how all businesses function. But I'm not a desk person; I can't sit. I need to move. So, I started working at the restaurant.

My father made me start as a dishwasher and then a prep cook. I learned the whole operation, front to back.

I had already learned the front of the house, the point of service aspect of things, but he wanted me to learn everything, from start to finish.

I'd rather stay in the kitchen all day than work on the floor or manage everything else, but that's not my choice. I do what's needed. I do a little of everything. On Tuesdays, I make pizzas with my father. Tuesday, Thursday, Saturday, I bake the bread for focaccia, croissants, cookies, tiramisu, you name it, there's nothing I don't do.

My sister does the pastries, which is awesome. She does an amazing job. She focuses on that. And then I kind of do the rest.

My first love with food was making bread. I started making bread when I was seventeen, and now I'm twenty-eight. But I also like making specialty dishes, because anytime it's something special, it means my father's taught me how to make it personally.

My dad cooked for us Monday to Saturday, and mom cooked on Sundays, so all week we'd eat Italian, and then on Sunday, more midwestern type food like chili. In school, my dad always made me lunch, which even made the teachers jealous. They'd say, "Oh my god. I'll buy you the school lunch if I can have the tomato, basil, and pasta in your thermos. Sometimes, I'd do it. But as I got older, I realized what was in my thermos was much better than what I could buy at the cafeteria.

Whenever I ate at a friend's house, their parents would always preface it by saying, "Now it's not going to be as good as your father's." I would always say, "Don't worry. I'm just happy to be here." But every single parent would say the same thing. Everybody knew my dad's cooking.

His biggest influence on me is how he treats people. My father's super passionate. Everyone can lose their head from time to time, and when he does, it's not pretty. But the way he treats people, he'll see someone who has had a long day, or doesn't really have enough money, or has had a rough year. I remember one day a friend of his came over. Everything had gone south for this guy. So, my dad made him a plate of spaghetti with clams, and sent them home with meats, cheeses, and a loaf of bread. For him, just the aspect of cooking is more like nourishment.

The only thing I would ever change is maybe limit the menu a bit more. As for the restaurant, I wouldn't change a thing. It has its own personality and charisma. I wouldn't update it or make it modern. I would never do that. For my father, it's a legacy thing. I was lucky enough to be born into this beautiful family, and the things my mother and father have both done to get the restaurant to where it is now. I wouldn't dare tarnish it. One reason I would keep this place as it is, would be to preserve the memory of my father and mother, and the hard work they put in to create something special.

My dad never asks for too much, and we all understand that whatever he wants goes because it's his place. He always orders the fish himself. We get our cans of tomatoes directly from Italy. I think it's why our food tastes so good. But we have to order it in advance.

People don't know how hard it is to run a restaurant, or how hard it is to create a successful restaurant. There's no other place in the world like Andreoli's. My father's always been the real deal. What he does is unparalleled. The food, what he makes, like the guanciale, the porchetta, how he does the fish, the pasta, and the way he does the bread. There's no other place like it. There are restaurants that are known for their pasta, or their steaks, or their fish. But my father does it all. What he does and what he's created is like one-of-a-kind.

There's a lot of pride in what we do at Andreoli. When somebody tells you the food and the experience were amazing, and the service was great. It feels better knowing that somebody enjoyed my sister's pastries or the dish my dad made. Everyone who works at Andreoli is kind of like family. It's nice to see that everyone's taking as much pride as we are. There's nothing more valuable than somebody who enjoys the food. We're not here just to make money. If that were the case, then prices would be doubled or tripled, and we'd be doing a completely different menu.

There's always something I tell servers or training staff, whenever you come to Andreoli: forget what you know about Italian food because this is completely different. Everything my dad does is as authentic as it gets. People who come here from Italy, this place is like home. This isn't just another Italian restaurant; this is the Italian restaurant.

Finally, none of this, Andreoli, the earlier restaurants,

my papa coming to America, would not have happened without my beautiful mom, Linda.

Linda Scorzo

People always ask how we ended up in Arizona. My oldest sister's husband was in the military, stationed in Arizona. I came to visit her, and the orange blossoms were in bloom. It was beautiful and I liked it there. I'm from a town in Missouri of less than 10,000 people. My college, Arizona State University (ASU), had 40,000 people. So, I moved to Arizona, and three months after I got here, my sister and her husband relocated to Las Vegas, so I'm out here by myself.

I'd studied a little French and Spanish in high school. Nothing formal, but it was on my transcript, so when I went ASU, I wanted to continue to learn a foreign language. This summer program came up to go to Italy, so I enrolled to learn Italian, and that's how I ended up strolling along in Florence the day Giovanni saw me with my girlfriend from college.

That was 1985 when Giovanni entered my life. I wanted to finish my degree and had two more years to go, followed by internships at Intel and E.F. Hutton, where I got my first job. So, I was already living and working in Arizona. Giovanni came to join me, and we got married. Neither of us really ever thought about going back to Italy, or going back to Missouri. I was happy with the way things were going here.

Life intervened as it does. Restaurant opportunities, too good to pass up, came along in Santa Fe, then San

Francisco. Weighing all of that against the best place to raise the children, somehow always brought us back to Arizona.

For example, at Babbo Ganzo restaurant in Santa Fe, Giovanni found faster success there. He was getting a following very quickly. Much quicker than La Bruschetta, which was very seasonal. Things died off on the vine in June in Arizona. Customers were nil in the summer and so whatever you made in the winter, you have to save for the summer. At one point we decided, let's stay with Santa Fe, so Francesca and I started to stay five days over there, a week over in Arizona, so we could start looking for a house over there. But a small adobe shack, around a thousand square feet, was a quarter of a million dollars back then, and it needed a lot of repairs. This was like a real peak time in Santa Fe for real estate. I suppose it was because it had become kind of a Hollywood sanctuary.

Then I got pregnant with Gian Paul. The woman who delivered Francesca was in Arizona, so I stayed with the doctor I knew. I didn't have a doctor in Santa Fe. I never thought about having the baby in Santa Fe for whatever reason. I was concerned Giovanni wasn't going to make it home for Gian Paul's delivery, but he did. He was here.

Once Gian Paul was born, I had an infant and a two-year-old, and it was too hard to travel back and forth. I had a home here, and I wasn't going to live in an apartment that didn't have what we needed. So, we agreed that Giovanni would be the one commuting now. And so that's what he did until the San Francisco opportunity came up, and we all moved there for a couple of years.

Fast forward to 1995, I moved our family from Scottsdale to San Francisco to help with Zingari. My mom helped us move and drove a 24-foot U-Haul with our Scottsdale furniture, while I followed behind in my car with a trailer hitched to the back. The trailer even had a window for the dogs and in my back seat my two kids, Francesca and Gian Paul listened to Barney songs for eighteen hours straight. We decided to drive straight through, other than to stop and let the dogs out, et cetera. As we drove across the Bay Bridge, I remembered that there had been an earthquake the year before. I prayed, please don't let there be another one right now. But we get there, making our way up and down through the hilly streets of San Francisco with no navigation, no GPS to 501 Post Street.

We scrambled to adjust to running a food operation for a hotel, the pace was hectic. In the middle of it, God blessed us with another son, Angelino, born October 1996.

When it came time to enroll Francesca in school and the options were so dismal and expensive, none of it felt right for her future. That's when we decided to move back to Arizona, where our home was still waiting for us.

This time I flew back.

Giovanni would commute back and forth for a while until we worked out another restaurant option in Arizona. Giovanni decided he should be here with us permanently. We've been here ever since.

I am so very proud of Giovanni and of our family. His talent continues to inspire me, and together we've built a life that is rich with love, hard work and meaning. I feel truly blessed and grateful for the journey we share and the life we live!

Sugo di Carne
(Meat Sauce)

PREP TIME: 20 MINUTES | COOK TIME: 2 HOURS
MAKES 4 - 6 SERVINGS

INGREDIENTS:

800 grams (g) ground beef (65%)

350 g ground pork (65%)

100 g pancetta, chopped finely

100 g carrots, chopped finely by hand

100 g celery, chopped finely by hand

100 g white onion, chopped finely by hand

1 tsp tomato paste

1.5 kilos Italian Whole Peeled San Marzano Tomatoes, pured*

6 oz Italian red wine

34 oz vegetable broth

Tomato sauce

4 oz whole milk

Salt and pepper

METHOD:

Chef recommends preparing/assembling ingredient list before starting to cook.

*Tomato Puree: Open the canned tomatoes. Using a large bowl and strainer (rest the strainer on top of the bowl, allowing the tomato juice to pour through). Using your hands, break open each tomato, removing the seeds, (tomato seeds are caught by the strainer). Add the remaining tomato pulp to the tomato juice. Throw away tomato seeds. Now with a hand-held mixer or food wand, puree the tomatoes and tomato juice.

Finely chop the onion, carrot, celery and pancetta, and set aside.

In a 2-quart pot, sauté pancetta over a medium heat. When the pancetta is almost cooked add the olive oil. Two minutes later, add the carrots, celery and onions to the pot. Sauté for approximately 15 minutes, careful to not burn the onions, until they get a golden-brown color (may need to reduce heat to medium low.) Now add the ground meat to the pot and cook for 20 minutes more. Now add the red wine. When the wine evaporates (approximately 3 to 5 minutes), add the tomato paste, and sauté for 5 more minutes.

Now add the tomato puree and cook for 2 hours, at a medium heat or just under. It is not necessary to cover the sauce.

Add the milk, salt and pepper to your liking.

Rinascere – Be Reborn!

CHAPTER 8
The King's Table

Like Francesca said, there's a table in Andreoli, tucked away near the fridge, that's become something of a legend. My daughter says it's what makes Andreoli's different. And Andreoli's wouldn't be Andreoli's without it. She may be right.

We call it the King's Table. Not because I'm a king—but because that table rules everything.

That's where I've heard stories from customers who've been coming for fifteen years. Where travelers from Italy sit and shake their heads and say, "This is better than back home." Where critics become friends, and strangers become family.

That's where I've watched kids grow up. Watched couples turn into parents. Watched people cry over pasta because it tasted like something they thought they'd lost.

That table has heard more truth than any Yelp page ever will. And if you listen closely, it'll talk to you.

It'll tell you about the man who walked away from a five-star kitchen to chase a girl across the ocean. It'll tell you about the woman who gave up comfort for conviction—and helped build something unforgettable.

It'll tell you about long nights, small victories, stubborn recipes, and the kind of love that doesn't need to be pretty to be real.

Because this story—this whole book—it isn't about food, not really. It's about belonging. Food is just the language we use to say, "You matter. Sit down. Stay a while."

Maybe I tell you "no" more than you're used to. Maybe you don't get a laminated menu or a side of ranch.

But if you walk through my door with an open heart—hungry for something honest—I promise you this: You'll leave full, with a smile on your face and probably a funny story to share.

Come and meet me at the King's Table.

Ci vediamo!

Bollito di Manzo
(Boiled Beef)

PREP TIME: 20 MINUTES | COOK TIME: 3 HOURS
MAKES 4 - 6 SERVINGS

INGREDIENTS:

2 ¼ lbs. chuck roast

3 – 4 feet butcher's twine (rope)

2 medium white onions – skin removed, leave whole

3 pieces of celery stalk

4 bay leaves

2 medium carrots (peeled, remove ends)

1 medium bunch of thyme

1 little bunch of Italian parsley

20 whole cloves

20 g salt

34 ounces of filtered water

Black pepper

METHOD:

Chef recommends preparing/assembling the ingredient list before starting to cook.

Take the onion and pierce the cloves into the onion flesh - 10 cloves per onion. Tie the bay leaves and thyme together with a twine so that it's easy to discard later.

In a large pot, add the water, onions, celery and carrots. Once you have added the vegetables to the water add the salt and pepper and bring to a boil.

In the meantime, clean and prepare the roast. Remove the chuck roast from the packaging, and wash with cold water. Pat the roast dry with paper towels. This will help the butcher's twine to adhere better to the roast. Lay the roast on a clean surface, fat side up.

Starting on one end, slide the twine under one end reaching the other end of the roast, tie a firm knot on the top of the roast (not so tight that it cuts into the meat) tight enough to secure the twine in place.

Now make loops every 1½ inches. Starting at one end of roast, slide twine under making evenly spaced loops along the entire length of the roast. Once you've reached the end of the roast, flip it over. Run the twine lengthwise down the center, weaving under each loop.

Option: Most butchers will tie a roast for you or you can purchase a premade net. After you are done, when the water starts to boil, add the meat. Cook at a medium high heat for 3 hours. Remove the roast to a cutting board, and strain and save the broth.

To Serve: Remove the twine from the roast, cut into half inch thick slices. Add to a serving dish, ladle broth over meat and garnish with fresh parsley.

Optional: You can also serve with boiled potatoes and carrots.

Rinascere – Be Reborn!

An alternate way to serve the Bollito is with Salsa Verde. It would be a lottery food combination!

Ladle a small amount of broth onto a warm dish.

Place a half inch thick slice of the roast on top, and generously spread the Salsa Verde over the meat.

Salsa Verde
(Green Sauce)

PREP TIME: 20 MINUTES | COOK TIME: 2 HOURS
MAKES 4-6 SERVINGS

INGREDIENTS:

2 eggs boiled

60 g bread (firm)

20 capers cured in vinegar – finely chopped

2 tsp white wine vinegar

2 garlic cloves (medium size) - finely chopped

4 anchovy filet (Italian) – finely chopped

140 g Italian parsley – finely chopped

120 g Italian extra virgin olive oil

Sea salt and pepper

METHOD:

Place eggs in a small pot. Add enough water to cover the eggs by ½ inch. Bring to a boil and continue to boil for 10 minutes. Remove from stove and immerse eggs in cold water. Wait 10 minutes to peel eggs.

In the meantime, put the inside of an Italian loaf of bread (don't include the crust) in a bowl and the vinegar. Take the stem out of the garlic cloves and finely chop. Add anchovy filets to chopping board and continue chopping. Add capers and finely chop. Add these items to a mixing bowl. Now pull stems from parsley stalks, hand chop leaves only, very finely, add to mixture.

Now back to eggs, crack and peel hard boiled eggs. Separate yolk from the white. Now pass the yolk only through a colander. Add to mixture.

In a separate bowl, whisk, extra virgin olive oil, salt and pepper together. Add to the mixture. Stir.

For a fine beautiful sauce.

Rinascere – Be Reborn!

CHAPTER 9
Tell Me What You Eat, And I Will Tell You Who You Are

In my opinion, the soul of a person is nourished first and foremost within the mother's womb by her love and the food she chooses to eat, then by her breast milk, and blossoms throughout the rest of life by the gift of their body to our Lord Jesus Christ. It's not just about following the Ten Commandments—it's about living by what I call the Eleventh: "Tell me what you eat, and I will tell you who you are."

I believe food deserves respect. Too often in America, food is just something to shovel in. It's fast, it's careless, and people barely taste it. And the so-called Italian food? It's not just different—it's wrong. Take spaghetti and meatballs—Americans serve it all together, sauce and all. In Italy, that's not how it's done. In the north, meatballs are served without sauce—maybe with lemon. In the south, like where I'm from, meatballs come with tomato, but we eat the pasta with sauce first, and the meatballs after as a second course, with roasted potatoes, green beans, or salad. Some things just aren't meant to be mixed.

I also see people come into my restaurant and ask for marinara sauce on their pasta. In Italy, there is no such thing as marinara sauce for pasta. In Italy, marinara is used only on pizza. But in America, they have turned a pizza toping into a pasta sauce—blasphemy!

And then there is Cacciucco—a seafood stew from Livorno. To do it right, you need the local fish. The exact ones. You can't get those in America, so when I see Cacciucco on a menu here, I already know it's going to be a disaster. You simply can't fake it.

The ingredients really do matter, for example the marinara they make in America is American. In most American Italian restaurants, they cook the marinara with this American Oregano, which is very stinky and bitter. When you smell the American Oregano, then smell the Italian oregano, there is no comparison. I only use Italian oregano in my marinara pizza sauce. We use either the plants or oregano that I get straight from Italy.

Now, let's talk about tomatoes. I only use tomatoes from Italy. People tell me to try the Jersey tomato. I try it. It's okay—but no big deal. Even tomatoes from Mexico are better than what's grown in the U.S. When I make sauce with Italian tomatoes, it stays smooth and non-acidic. If I use an American tomato—even from a jar—it's too acidic and toxic.

One guy I knew brought tomato seeds from Napoli to Napa Valley.

"It's the same soil," he said. "Try it."

I did. "Disgusting," I told him.

"But I'll give them to you for free," he said.

"No," I said. "I don't want them even for free."

You can't fake good tomatoes. You can't fake good soil.

The dish that's always in my mind is my grandmother's tomato sauce. I only make it at the restaurant when I'm in the mood and thinking of her. It's simple—onion, or sometimes just tomato, a little pepper, and Parmigiano. You don't mess it up with cream or margarine. It's all about the purity of the tomato.

I also remember when she made roast pork or sausage on skewers from the mirto plant, which grows wild in Calabria and Sardinia. That aroma is in my bones. That's what I carry in my food.

And bread—don't get me started. I wanted the best bread in the world. So, I went back to Cetraro thirty years ago and found a bakery with a 120-year-old starter. That's what we use. That starter has music inside. We only use purified water and the best flour.

There's another thing in America that I will not do and that's make a dish a certain way just because that's the way the customer wants it. You may recall that from when I turned down making Florentine steak for the food critic's husband. Here's another example. One day, this guy came into the restaurant and asked for a sandwich with eggplant, prosciutto, capicollo, and salame.

"Sir, this is no good for me," I told him.

"What do you mean?" he asked.

"I don't make it."

"Well, I like it," he said.

"I don't care if you like it, I don't like it," I said. "Who's the doctor—me or you?"

"Well, I'm from New York," he said. "In New York, they do whatever I say."

"Well, I'm not in New York."

"But I pay," he insisted. Some Americans think they own everything. The streets, the restaurants, even the food. But not in my restaurant.

"I have a line behind you," I told him. "You don't have to eat here."

"Somebody else here cooked for me this year," he said.

So, I called the guys from the kitchen. "Hey, come outside." I pointed to him. "You know this guy?"

No one did. I turned back to him.

"Sir, you're a liar. Now, do you want to eat or leave?"

"Okay," he said. "I'll take it your way."

The thing is, when I tell someone something doesn't belong, they usually still want it. Like clams with Parmigiano. I say no.

They say, "But I like it. I'm American, I do what I want."

"Not in my restaurant," I say. "If your doctor tells you, it's your heart, do you argue it's your liver? Of course not. I'm like that doctor. You either listen or eat somewhere else. Some say I'm mean. I don't care. In my restaurant, you will have respect for the food."

One time, a popular TV host wanted me to come back

on his show. He asked me to combine pork ribs with sour gummy bears. I'd already been on his show three times.

"You can do this," he said.

"I can, but I won't," I told him.

"But that's the idea—it's funny."

I didn't think it was funny. I thought it was criminal. These cooking shows are full of people making garbage and judges saying, "If it were me, I'd add this or that." What they need to do is disappear. You can't put bubblegum with tomato and basil. You should go to jail for that. Twenty years minimum. (Okay—maybe I'm exaggerating. But you get the point.)

There's a big difference between food culture in America and in Italy. In Italy, you had to work for years before you were considered a chef. In America, you go to school for two years and become an "executive chef." Most of them don't know anything. They know how to put food on a plate, not how to taste. They grew up on barbecue sauce, McDonalds, Burger King, and peanut butter and jelly. That's their flavor memory.

I used to train apprentices from culinary schools in New York and San Francisco. I'd say, "Sue your school. You don't know anything. Your mother spent two hundred thousand dollars so some criminal could teach you this?" But no one says anything. Everyone smiles and nods.

I went to culinary school in high school back in Italy. If there's one thing I understand about culinary school, it's that they're kind of worthless. You can go to the best university in the world, but if you're a donkey, when you get out, you're still going to be a donkey. My father went to third grade. My father can build a house.

When somebody practices with food, or with anything, it's more than what you learn from school. The culinary school I went to teaches you stuff, but mostly it's a mix of different things, like language, how to organize a kitchen, how to order, and how to count the percentage of the food you use. They teach you decoration. I like decoration, but only up to a certain point. But decorations are more like paintings than food, but I prefer food to paintings. I don't go to a restaurant because it has a million-dollar chandelier. No, I go for the food. I can go to a restaurant without the windows, but the food—that's what's important. In America, they'll tell you to go to a restaurant because it has a nice aquarium inside, or a beautiful chandelier. I don't really give a damn about those things. I like simplicity. Simplicity. It's my goal. Originality. It's my other goal.

Sometimes you go into a restaurant that says it's Italian American. I don't know what that is. For me, Italian American doesn't exist. If it did, it would be, you go in and they cook hamburgers, hot dogs, chicken wings, and then some Italian dishes. Then it would be Italian and American. Maybe, when they say Italian American, they mean it's Americanized. But I don't think even that exists, because to say Americanized, it's not really Italian. They just say that because they don't really know how to cook Italian.

Once, Linda and I offered to cook lunch at our kids' school. They turned us down. They were happy giving kids peanut butter and jelly sandwiches. That broke my heart.

I've tried hard to change how people think about food. Through this book, I hope current and future generations in America learn to love food the way I did—through respect, tradition, and family. I was lucky to be raised with real food and real love around the table. And now, I'm doing everything I can to pass that on.

My son Gian Paul was thinking he wanted to open another restaurant, and he said to me one time, "Papa, hey, we'll just put a guy there, give him a recipe, that's all you need."

My wife agreed, "Yes, he's right. They can do what you do."

I say, "No, don't kid yourself. They can't do anything I'm doing simply with a recipe!" I agree with Pellegrino Artusi, one of Italy's greatest gastronomes: there is no such thing as a correct recipe. There are simply too many variables—potatoes, flour, eggs, temperature, humidity. A good dish isn't just about a recipe. It's about memory. It's about care. It's about orgasm.

My father always said the truth hurts, and I just happen to be brutally honest, so if you ask me a question, be prepared to hear the truth.

I tell the truth about how Americans eat. In America, anywhere you go, there is a McDonalds, here, McDonalds there. Fifty states in America, and there are McDonalds in all of them. Tens of thousands of McDonalds. Are those people putting up McDonalds everywhere, somebody who is in love with food? No! They don't have any idea what real food is.

When I talk about those smells, they get stuck to your brain, and they will never go away. What I'm saying here, is for kids, what smells and tastes are you putting in their brain? You train your child's brain to understand food if you give them beautiful foods, not garbage foods. For example, I can cook Chinese food better than some Chinese restaurants.

Did I cook Chinese growing up? No, but I developed a refined sense of taste and smell. I can. I taste everything. Your brain is developed how to taste from the time you're a baby. Now. I haven't been a taster of a lot of different wine before, but when distributors bring me wine to taste, they can come one day later, and I know the taste without looking at the wine. I remember smells perfectly from fifty years ago. As I make the dishes like the Fava Bean soup, I'm right back in Italy in my mother's arms.

When we traveled back to Italy for the summer when my children were young, my son Angelino would wake up first thing in the morning, and say, "Papa, can you smell the peppers?" I think my daughter Francesca has my nose. Angelino next.

People talk about Italian cuisine like it's some sacred, unchanging thing. Let me tell you something: We stole half of it.

Tomatoes? Not Italian. They came from the Americas. Polenta? Maize. Same story.

Even wine—the thing we're supposedly born with in our blood—came from grapes first cultivated in the Middle East. But here's the trick: we perfected it.

We took a few basic, humble ingredients—flour, olive oil, water, salt—and made magic. Not because we were born special. But because we had no choice.

I believe Italy is blessed. There are stories that Jesus stopped in Italy and I believe it. He placed in Italy as a gift for all—the most beautiful olive oil and other things, for this love of food and family. Anywhere you go, it's blessed in wine, in vinegar, in olives, everything. In a little country the size of California.

Now they try to replicate Italy in California. I tried to find something close to the same thing in California with the tomatoes, the wine, and other things. It's just not the same. In Napa Valley, it's all the same land. In Italy, in my town, the wine my father makes from grapes, the next town doesn't grow. We have bio-diverse climates in Italy. The climates from Africa affect Italy. That's why in Sicily they grow banana, papaya, mango, and the best avocados. In Sicily they also grow the best Bronte pistachio. The best bergamot comes from Calabria. The best lemon and radicchio from the Amalfi Coast. Why are they the best? . . . because in Italy, we compete with who has the best . . . who makes the best? And we have the perfect soil to make everything.

And that's why I think Italy is really blessed, not by politics or power, but for everything else. But in Italy, people are raised with good taste, they understand the connection between taste, food, family and love. In Italy, a doctor would teach you to eat the best. If you go to a doctor here and say you have a problem with your heart, they give you a prescription. I believe Italy is blessed ... Jesus stopped in EBOLI, Italy.

Italy isn't built on luxury. It's built on scraps. When you grow up with nine people around the table, one chicken to share, and a war outside your window, you learn to stretch. You learn to create. You learn to turn limitations into flavors.

That's what I did. I didn't go to culinary school. I didn't have a résumé full of starred restaurants. What I had was a childhood filled with women who cooked with instinct, men who grew things with their hands, and a family that taught me you don't serve anything you wouldn't eat yourself. That's the difference. That's the mindset.

So, when I came to America and saw people smothering pasta in Alfredo sauce, calling overcooked spaghetti and meatballs "authentic," or serving risotto with regular rice, I didn't get angry. I got focused. Because this isn't about borders. It's about standards.

I'm somebody who loves food, and if it's not good, I leave it. Sometimes I'm unhappy with what I cook. I have an unhappy moment because I make a recipe that doesn't come out the way I want. Like when I made something, and I missed something. But I talked to Jesus. Then it came to me in my brain, and I did it again, and it was perfect. I thought oh my God, you understand me with this recipe. I felt so happy, I started to sing victoriously.

You don't have to be born in Italy to understand what Italian food really is. You just have to respect it. Cook slow. Use good ingredients. Don't cheat. Don't drown it in nonsense. Let the product speak.

Same thing with life. You don't need everything to be perfect. You don't need wealth. You don't need fancy equipment or ten investors or a TikTok marketing strategy. You need conviction. You need discipline. You need to take what's in front of you—whatever it is—and make something beautiful out of it. That's what we've always done. That's what I've done.

If you ask me what it means to be Italian, I won't tell you it's about passport stamps or fluency in Dante. I'll tell you it's about showing up hungry . . . and never, ever wasting the meal.

Rigatoni alla Amatriciana
(Rigatoni with Guanciale, Tomato and Pecorino)

PREP TIME: 15 MINUTES | COOK TIME: 10 - 15 MINUTES
MAKES 4 SERVINGS

INGREDIENTS:

17.6 oz (500g) Rigatoni – Italian Imported brand

5 ¼ oz Guanciale – cut into ¼ inch cubes

3 cups Italian Whole Peeled San Marzano Tomatoes, pureed*

*Tomato Puree: Open the canned tomatoes. Using a large bowl and strainer (rest the strainer on top of the bowl, allowing the tomato juice to pour through). Using your hands, break open each tomato, removing the seeds, (tomato seeds are caught by the strainer). Add the remaining tomato pulp to the tomato juice. Throw away tomato seeds. Now with a hand-held mixer or food wand, puree the tomatoes and tomato juice.

2 ½ tsp. salt

½ tsp. crushed pepperoncino (dried chili pepper)

1 cup Imported Pecorino Romano – grated

METHOD:

Chef recommends preparing/assembling ingredient list

before starting to cook.

Fill a large pot with water. Bring it to a boil.

Take a large iron skillet (12 inches), place on high heat. Once pan is heated, add the cubed guanciale. Sautee and stir, lower to medium heat, cook until crispy golden brown, be careful not to burn it. Once down, turn off heat. Move crispy guanciale to an 8-inch sauté pan. You're going to continue to use the iron skillet, do not remove any fat.

Using that iron skillet, turn the heat on medium, add the pepperoncino, sauté for 30 seconds. Add the tomato puree, and 1 ½ teaspoons of salt and simmer on medium heat for 15 minutes. Turn off the heat. Stir in ½ cup pecorino cheese, mix well.

Now, you need to cook the pasta. Add 1 ¼ teaspoon of salt to boiling water, then add the pasta. Cook 9 - 10 minutes for al dente.

Timing tip: After sauce is has cooked for 10 minutes, cook your pasta.

Strain the pasta, save a little water (½ cup). Add the pasta to the sauce, mix well.

Simultaneously, warm up the guanciale in its pan.

Serving Instructions: Transfer the pasta to a large serving platter. Sprinkle with warm guanciale evenly over the top. Finish with sprinkling the remaining ½ cup pecorino over the entire dish.

CHAPTER 10
My Vision for the Future

Let me tell you something I've learned after decades of feeding people: Some people just won't get it. They'll walk into my restaurant, see the chalkboard menu, and ask, "Where's the lasagna?" They'll order carbonara and ask for a side of garlic bread. They'll taste the eggplant and say, "It's good, but could use more cheese." These people don't want food— they want validation. They want the food to be familiar; to match some image they've built in their heads. And when it doesn't, they say it's wrong. But it's not wrong. It's just not what they know.

That's the thing about real food. It challenges you. It speaks its own truth. And not everyone wants to hear it. People leave reviews sometimes that say, "He wouldn't make it how I wanted."

Correct. You don't walk into a tailor and demand he cuts your suit like a hoodie. This isn't Burger King. You don't get it your way. You get it my way. The right way.

I've had people walk out. I've had people write nasty things online. I've had critics call me difficult. I don't care.

Because the people who do get it? The ones who sit down, take a bite, and say nothing—not because they're unhappy, but because they're busy feeling something—those people come back. They bring friends. They become family.

So if you're reading this book and you're irritated—if you're rolling your eyes and muttering that I sound too proud, too stubborn, too intense—let me give you some advice: Read it again. Because maybe what's bothering you isn't the story—maybe it's the mirror. Maybe you're used to compromise. Maybe you've stopped asking for excellence. Maybe you've accepted the microwave and forgotten what fire tastes like. I'm not here to make you comfortable. I'm here to make you remember.

That's why we are very busy now, at Andreoli. But even now, it's not like every night we are busy. There are other restaurants, who in my mind are run by criminals, that are busier than mine, even though they belong in jail, the owners. I sometimes wonder, "What's wrong with this country?" But the thing is, Americans, how they grow up, I think they have to eat a variety of different foods every week. If I go to Italy and I like one restaurant, I'm finished. America is different. Tonight Japanese, tomorrow Vietnamese, next day Polish, next day Mexican.

Every few months, someone says to me, "You should expand. Open another location. Franchising is the move!" And I say the same thing every time: "No." Not because I'm afraid. Not because I don't know how. Not because the money wouldn't be nice. But because this restaurant—this one, imperfect, chaotic, beautiful place—is already more than enough.

You know why most chefs open second and third restaurants? Because they're trying to escape the kitchen. They want to be "visionaries." They want to be seen. I don't want to be seen. I want to cook. That's what this has always been about. The flame. The pot. The product. The plate. Not spreadsheets. Not "brand alignment." Not influencer partnerships. Just the food. I see these restaurants now, covered in neon, blasting music, with menus that read like TikTok trends. It's not food anymore. It's a photo op. They serve "experiences." I serve a meal.

I'm not one of those chefs that use his talents to make his dish look like art. I prefer to spend time with taste and flavor. I'm not chasing a Michelin star. If I want to see art, I'll go to a museum or an art gallery.

At Andreoli, we don't have gimmicks. We don't have theme nights. We don't have seven pages of fusion nonsense. We have one dish made right. Then another. Then another. Because fire still matters. Technique still matters. Conviction still matters.

I don't care if the world is moving faster. I'm not chasing it. I'm building something that stays. You want to know what the future is? It's not a thousand restaurants. It's one—done the right way. That's my future. And if I've done this right, it's yours too.

Pappardelle con Costine di Maiale
(Pappardelle with Pork Short Ribs)

PREP TIME: 35 MINUTES | COOK TIME: 2 HOURS 55 MINUTES
MAKES 6 SERVINGS

INGREDIENTS:

3 cloves garlic

1 large red onion

1/2 cup extra-virgin olive oil

3 ¼ pounds pork ribs (cut into individual sections, every 2 inches)

Three 800-gram cans Italian peeled tomatoes (pureed recipe below)

16 ounces Italian Pinot Grigio

2 bay leaves

100 grams sea salt, plus additional as needed

Freshly ground black pepper

2 pounds pappardelle pasta

1 cup grated Locatelli Pecorino cheese

METHOD:

Tomato Puree: Open the canned tomatoes. Using a large bowl and strainer (rest the strainer on top of the bowl, allowing the tomato juice to pour through). Using

your hands, break open each tomato, removing the seeds, (tomato seeds are caught by the strainer). Add the remaining tomato pulp to the tomato juice. Throw away tomato seeds. Now with a hand-held mixer or food wand, puree the tomatoes and tomato juice.

Finely chop the garlic and onions and sauté in the olive oil over medium heat, making sure not to smoke the olive oil, and cooking the garlic and onions until golden. Add the short ribs to the pan and brown, turning occasionally, for 20 minutes.

Meanwhile, crush the Italian peeled tomatoes into a bowl using the tomato recipe above. Add the Pinot Grigio to the pan and let the wine evaporate, then add the tomatoes along with the bay leaves and 1 cup water. Cook, while stirring occasionally, over low to medium heat for 2 hours. [Partially covered. At a low simmer, until ribs are tender] Add salt and pepper.

Remove the ribs from the sauce and remove the meat from the bone. Return the meat to the sauce and dispose of the bones.

Meanwhile, boil a pot of slightly salted water. Boil the pappardelle for 7 to 8 minutes, or to desired consistency. Strain the pasta, then place in a large bowl. Add meat and sauce and stir the ingredients to combine. Sprinkle Locatelli Pecorino Romano on top of the dish. Add additional fresh ground pepper to taste.

Happy Customers and the Dishes That Make Them Happy

There was this movie, *When Harry Met Sally*, where the actress playing Sally pretends to have an orgasm in a deli, and this lady at another table turns to her waiter and says, "I'll have what she's having." I had something similar happen. This lady came up to me after her meal and said my dish gave her an orgasm. The point is the food was orgasmic. I have an orgasm making it. When I bring the food out, especially to my friends from Italy, they know. I don't just serve the food, I want to be excited for what they say, and what they say makes me very, very happy.

Linda—my brilliant wife, business partner, and love of my life—asked some of our customers to share their stories about Andreoli, and even about meeting me. I figured by now you've heard enough from me, so how about a few stories from the people on the other side of the counter?

Chris Campbell

Our dear friend Chris Campbell walked in one day looking for a paint approval (we were having the restaurant painted) and walked out with a sandwich and a lifelong friendship. Here's what he had to say:

I first met Giovanni when he and Linda were opening Andreoli's. I was working for the Property Owners Association at the time. Giovanni came in the office and was ready for a fight. Apparently, he and Linda had been having trouble getting the exterior paint color they wanted to use on the building approved because of a difficult employee. Said employee was not in the office when Giovanni came in, so I took his paint color sample to the Executive Director who immediately signed the approval. Giovanni was surprised how easy the process was and thanked me. I told him that I really had nothing to do with the approval other than taking it to the correct person, but Giovanni pretty much ignored me. He told me to come into the restaurant the following week when they were open and he would buy me a sandwich. What was a random initial interaction has turned into a friendship which is highly valued by not only me, but my family as well.

I can distinctly remember each time Giovanni made me a dish for the first time; there are really too many memories to pick out one or two to mention. What has always stood out to me is the passion for food that Giovanni has and how important it is to him to share that passion with others. I believe he does this out of his altruistic nature; he wants others to enjoy food the way he does. I have always been amazed how he can take the most basic ingredients and turn them into a masterpiece.

A very important memory I have is when my wife was pregnant with our first child. She had regular cravings for Tiramisu. Without fail, if I was in the restaurant, Giovanni would make sure that I always had an order of Tiramisu to take to my wife. I don't think he forgot once over the course of the entire pregnancy.

On one occasion, I walked into the kitchen at the restaurant and Giovanni was arguing with a produce delivery guy that he was not going to accept the carrots because they were bad. The delivery guy kept arguing that they were fine and that the delivery would have to be accepted. As I walked in, Giovanni gave me a carrot and told me to eat it and tell him what I thought. After I ate it, I said, "it tastes like a carrot." Giovanni said, "no, it tastes like dirt." As soon as he said that, I could taste the dirt. The delivery guy's face just fell and he took the carrots back.

Once Giovanni asked me if I liked fish. I told him that I did. Without any further discussion, he went to work. He kept telling me the name of the dish in Italian, but I could not understand him, so he finally told me the English translation of "crazy water." I don't remember the preparation of the dish taking more than just a few minutes but I remember how blown away I was with the flavor of the meal. It is always surprising to me how

Giovanni makes such amazing food so quickly and with what appears to be such little effort on his part.

Reading Chris's words reminds me of something important: I don't just love food—I love people. And having a restaurant has introduced me to some of the best people on Earth. Want a poetic take on Andreoli? Here's how our customer Oscar Contesini put it:

Oscar Contesini

There is a piece of Italian theatrical realism in Scottsdale, Arizona_Andreoli, where the real Italian lifestyle is staged. At Andreoli, Italian food is consumed—but more than that, it's a real-life experience: laughter, passion, conversation. Giovanni is the great puppeteer of this comedy, staged daily. Breakfast, lunch, dinner—it's always the same in rhythm, always different in soul. This isn't reality on stage. This is reality as the stage.

I couldn't have said it better. And then there's Stefano Spalvieri, who moved from France to Arizona in 2010. I'll let him tell it.

Stefano Spalvieri

At Giovanni's, it's Italy! We arrived from France in July 2010. Arizona was a whole new world. One day, passing by on the way to school, we found an Italian grocery store. That store became a second home. Giovanni won us over with his food, his warmth, and the true Italian atmosphere. His bread and croissants reminded us of France. He broadcast soccer games for the boys. Our daughter loved watching him sing and play piano. I was fascinated by his creativity in the kitchen. My husband and Giovanni became very close. Since we returned to France in 2013, we come back to Scottsdale every two years—just to see Giovanni and spend time at Andreoli. Thank you for all the dishes, pizzas, and long conversations. We love you!

This next couple is from Germany, who write me to share their favorite food experience, and what makes my recipes so special.

Georgina and Ingo

To Holy Giovanni we came, quite literally, like the Virgin Mary to the child. Tired of American food, we desperately sought a taste of European home—and we found it among family photos on the walls, the fear of sitting at the chef's table without enough appetite, and staff who eagerly, like a papal disciple awaiting salvation, offered their cheek for a slap.

And the food—well, it's more like a revelation than food and is never what's listed on the menu. That's why we love you, Giovanni. We love you anyway. Even if it's not always entirely clear if—or especially when—we'll make it out of your place alive.

But with you, we entered a lifelong bond with open eyes from the very first moment. And we have not regretted it for a single second. Carissimo amico, non vogliamo più fare a meno di te nemmeno per un secondo nella nostra vita. But if there's one thing we've learned above all: Never come to your restaurant in bad shoes, and never, ever dare to sprinkle salt over your spaghetti after the fact!

Roberto Felice

A great dish that stands out (though there are so many) is his lasagna. While it was absolutely fantastic in taste, what made it truly special was what it represented. I vividly recall the nights when he would make it at the restaurant, and at the end of the evening, we would all sit together to devour what was left. It wasn't just friends and workers at the table—he welcomed family as well. I remember seeing the children and spouses of employees join in, creating a warm, inclusive atmosphere.

That's Gianni for you: a giver at heart. He's always ready to help anyone, never worrying about what he might get in return.

I've been lucky to know him for nearly forty years, ever since I first met him at his aunt's restaurant in Gilroy. Over the years, I've worked with him, and I can confidently say he's one of the greatest chefs I've ever encountered. But more importantly, he's an incredible friend and a devoted family man.

Gianni's generosity, kindness, and dedication should serve as an example for today's youth. He has a way

of making everyone feel valued and welcome, and I'm grateful to have been part of his journey.

Vince Risi

I first met Giovanni Scorzo on Friday, November 3, 2017. He was sitting in a vintage Barber's chair outside the entrance of Andreoli's. I introduced myself to Giovanni and mentioned that I had just returned from New York, where I had tried various salumi at Mario Batali's Otto Enoteca. At that moment, Giovanni stopped the swiveling barber's chair and invited me inside to experience his homemade salumi and sausage selections. A few days later, Giovanni served me a special scallop dish. Since then, I have become addicted to Giovanni's cooking, which always conveys his passion for Italian culture and cuisine.

Mona Mensing

My food memory would have to start with Linda's pants. I met Linda at Kachina Country Day School in Paradise Valley, Arizona when our kids went there as kindergartners. Linda was beautiful. Linda is beautiful. No, I mean, like truly stunning in the most authentic and true way. In fact, when she showed up to help create a garden in the sliver of earth next to the school rooms toting a shovel, sporting the most incredible black and white Valentino pants, I thought, I think I love this woman.

This beauty was not afraid to get dirty, she loved it, like me. I think we both thought, in this world of Scottsdale mommies we were each a breath of fresh air. And so, we became friends. She told me about her husband, how he was "different"—Italian, he had his own way of thinking and doing things. Oh, how true that would become.

I met Giovanni at their house which was filled with love, food, and angels everywhere.

Giovanni was a presence. Giovanni is a presence. He was busy doing something in the kitchen and the kids were circling him, and all of them were speaking in a flurry of Italian. And, it was loud. Loud is my wheelhouse, and I was just drawn to them all.

Before we actually ate Gianni's food at their restaurant LeccaBaffi, we were privileged to hear one of the many philosophical ponderings that Giovanni would bestow on us when we sat down to chat. His disdain for fast food, for American style and food preparation was deep. And I agreed with him. I will never forget about the dish he told me he and his father would make using wild strawberries gathered from the side of the mountains in Calabria. They were so small and delicate they had to be gathered using a needle. That is love and honor of food.

Eating Gianni's food changed how I looked at food, how I thought about food, and of course, how I ate food. There are many occasions where I recognized that Giovanni's relationship with food is next level-it's spiritual.

The very first time my husband and I had a meal at LeccaBaffi was life changing for both of us. First, we were welcomed into the homey environment created by unique antique pieces and staff who were "family". The first thing I recall is the antipasto bar. There was an antique credenza with plates and plates of grilled vegetables. But these vegetables had so much flavor, and they were grilled to perfection. Just the idea of an antipasto bar thrilled me. The dish that we both recall that redefined our palette was the homemade taglierini with a mushroom sauce, Taglierini Aurora. There was something so savory, so warming and exciting as we ate this. The flavors simply delighted us, we kept looking at each other like—are you tasting this, is this the best thing you have ever eaten or what? Steve literally sopped up my dish and his with the crusty, earthy bread that of course, was homemade that morning. When it was time for dessert, we ordered tiramisu—I had never had tiramisu before. Could a desert be made from cloud linings, from the delicate gossamer of angel wings? Yes, that is Giovanni's tiramisu. I have had tiramisu since, and it never fails to fall short of the delicate ethereal flavors of Gianni's.

And, as the years passed, the restaurants changed, the home changed, but angels were always there. One night when we were eating at the restaurant, Steve mentioned that he had been diagnosed with a heart condition. Gianni whipped up a big plate of grilled onions telling him that they were good for his blood.

And, when our daughter was to become a bat mitzvah, there was no other food that I could think of that I wanted for the event. Catering was not something they did often, and I knew how special it was to have this for the event. Gianni created something really special for the people in attendance that night. I will never forget it.

That is the magic of Gianni's food—it speaks to the stomach, the head, and the heart.

To this day, I have not had better cappuccinos, better pasta, better combinations of sauces and meats and flavors in my life than I have had at the restaurants and the home that Linda and Giovanni created.

Sometimes it is a member of the Andreoli family who get to experience customer stories that warm all of our hearts. This one is from Andreoli's front of the house operator.

Jeff Ricciardi

Jon and Kim have been coming to Andreoli for as long as I can remember. They are regular customers of Andreoli when they are visiting from Canada. Jon and Kim enjoy pastas, wine and prime cuts of meat when they dine with us. They typically end their dinners with decaf coffee and dessert.

On one visit, Jon share with me that his mom was in hospice here in Scottsdale. This visit was to begin making end of life arrangements. Kim was in Canada and planned to join Jon in a couple of weeks. The next time Jon and Kim visited Andreoli, Jon shared that his mom had passed comfortably, surrounded by family. I offered my condolences, and then began to present our specials for the evening. That evening's menu featured a 2 ½ pound Bistecca Fiorentina. Giovanni had cut it personally earlier that day. Knowing that Jon and Kim typically like our prime NY and ribeye steaks, I offered the Bistecca Fiorentina. I explained that we would grill to a perfection for them. The Bistecca would be presented on a board with roasted potatoes and fennel baked with gruyere cheese. Jon and Kim were all smiles and placed the order and added two Zia Rosina salads to start.

I checked in on them, in the secluded pizza area room table that had requested. They had smiles like kids opening Christmas presents on Christmas Day when the special arrived. I went to their table again once they were finishing coffee and dessert. Jon and Kim shared with me that their evening and meal took them back to a meal they had in Torino a few years back. In that moment, they were taken back to a patio table in Torino sharing a fabulous Bistecca together like ours! Wow, what a compliment! Their sadness was replaced with joy because of our food. They continue to visit us when they are in town. They love our restaurant. They love our food and they love us for impacting their lives.

Jimmy Chase

Meeting Giovanni Scorzo in the mid-eighties when he walked into the Jewelry store I was running, was the beginning of our lifetime friendship. The salesperson that greeted him came to me and said, "I can't understand anything this man is saying, would you please see if you can help him?" Giovanni spoke very little English at the time and I spoke no Italian, yet we were instant friends. We shared a mutual love for collectible watches, cars, and of course the experience of food, as I learned of his new restaurant La Bruschetta in Scottsdale.

He introduced me to black squid, white asparagus, fresh anchovies, any number of internal organs, and the best calamari on the planet. I watched him butcher a pig and followed its journey, as it became ribs, sausage and prosciutto. It has been written that he is "the Pizza Nazi," and "He discriminates against non-Italians." Above all, he raised my passion for fine food to a higher level.

Once, while eating at Andreoli's, Giovanni overheard me mention that I have been to a different local restaurant. I felt as if I had been busted as I was confronted with "how was the restaurant?" As the blood drained from my face, the only seemingly safe reply that came to mind was "it was okay." To which Giovanni schooled me, "that's what's wrong with America's relationship with food. You will eat at a place because it has quick service, it's inexpensive, or it has a nice atmosphere. As he popped me on the back of my head he said, " it should always be about the food!" Now, even when in Italy, every restaurant is measured and compared to the culinary expertise of the great Chef Scorzo.

Over the decades, I watched this handsome, charming artist become a star, while remaining true to his convictions, as a husband, a father, and a real family man, who along with his beautiful wife Linda, raised their three wonderful children to become fine adults.

Besides his obvious passion for food and his unique sense of humor, his intoxicating zest for life has made being his friend, truly one the best blessings of my life.

Sta' zitto e mangia! ~Chef Giovanni Scorzo

Bill (Bob) Sichko

When we moved into our new home in 2015, Sherre and I would visit Italian delis and restaurants that we either came across by word of mouth or from just looking in the yellow pages. We must have visited at least twelve places, of which Andreoli's was one. At the same time, since we were new to the neighborhood, we decided to have an open house for our neighbors on New Year's Eve that year. In planning for that, Sherre & I wanted to have a number of traditional Italian offerings (antipasti plate, Lasagna, focaccia, etc.) and we decided to have one of the Italian places that we visited make some of the food for us. We both agreed that our first choice was Andreoli's.

I called shortly before Christmas and spoke with a young lady who introduced herself as Francesca, and gave her an order. I also recall her making a number of suggestions. In any event, I show up on New Year's Eve at noon, I meet Francesca, and she initially informs me there is no food order for Bill. Needless to say, I was a little concerned, so Francesca asked me what all I ordered, at which point, her eyes brightened up and said, I do have a similar order for a Bob, you look like a Bob, so you can have it. She assisted me with getting everything into the car and off I went.

On that day, the only person I met was Francesca. That evening, all the food was a hit. We decided then that if we wanted Italian food, Andreoli's was our number one choice, so we started going to the restaurant. I would always say hi to Francesca and told her my name was Bill, but she didn't care, she said it was Bob. Sometime in the next six months, she introduced me to Giovanni, and I told him how much I appreciated his food.

The next time I came, I brought him a bottle of wine to show my appreciation. My first interaction with Giovanni was pretty benign. As time passed, Sherre, Syl & I would come for dinner (Syl & Francesca struck up a friendship) and I would bring Giovanni a bottle of wine from time to time to show my appreciation. Sometime in 2018 or 2019, we came in and you all were really busy, and the wait was thirty minutes, maybe more. In any event, Francesca came over and told us we should call or text her before we come down, and she will ensure we have a table. We exchanged numbers, she also had Angelino give us his number and we started doing that. At the same time, Francesca (and sometimes Angelino) would text me when Giovanni was making something really special (Bistecca Florentine, Lasagna, ossobuco, rabbit, etc.) and asked if we wanted to come in, and if we did, she would have Giovanni save one or two orders for us. During this time, I was having more and more interaction with Giovanni. We talked about how my Mom's family was from Calabria, how much I enjoyed his cooking, and what foods I liked, we talked about family and other things.

October 2020, and I am flying home after being in Philadelphia on business for the week. When I land in Phoenix, there's a text from Angelino. He said Giovanni made some chicken liver pate, potatoes w/spicy peppers, risotto w/porcini mushrooms, rabbit and oxtail and asked him (Angelino) to see if I could stop by because he (Giovanni) knew how much I enjoyed rabbit. That was the beginning of many stops at Andreoli after landing at PHX.

In January 2021, for my 67th birthday, we ate dinner at Andreoli's. I still have the text I sent Angelino the next morning (at this time, I did not have Giovanni's number). Here's the text:

Angelino, please show this to your dad: Giovanni, THANK YOU for a PERFECT Birthday dinner. Sitting at that table with the garage door open and near the wood-burning oven made the atmosphere feel like we were in Italy. Printing the menu was a very nice touch, but what was on the menu was mouthwatering. The bruschetta, your father's peppers, the spicy potatoes, and the lamb chops. But the highlight was the food itself. DELICIOUS, DELICIOUS, SIMPLY DELICIOUS. One of the BEST meals Sherre & I have ever had, especially the seafood. I have eaten some really fresh seafood around the world (Italy, Brazil, Japan, Mexico, Thailand, Seattle, Vancouver, New Orleans) but the assortment you put together was so varied, so fresh and so, so tasty! I also very much appreciate you making your grandmother's sauce (Nonna Sofia). That was FABULOUS!! And PLEASE Thank Francesca for me. She "nailed" both cakes. She has some real talent for baking. They were really, really good. Most importantly though, I could taste the love in everything (including the cakes) and we feel so humbled, thankful, and blessed you & Francesca would take the time & effort. I also appreciate you having a grappa with me. Finally, please thank Rosario for the excellent service he gave us. THANK YOU, THANK YOU, THANK YOU. God Bless You & your family. You have given Sherre & I a wonderful experience that we will remember the rest of our lives.

April 2021 — Giovanni was Colonel Sanders that evening. The BEST fried chicken I ever had.

June 2022 — Giovanni sent me a very comforting and heartwarming text when our son Steven died. The next time I was at the restaurant (a few days after Steven's funeral), Giovanni along w/Francesca, Gian Paolo, and Angelino, came over and each gave me a hug. Giovanni then sat with me for some time (even though I had stopped by to get a small & quick takeout order), offered some very comforting words, and then proceeded to be so generous making me a BIG basket of goodies knowing that good food can be so comforting.

Feb 2023 — had 8 guests from Chicago. Giovanni made us crudo, octopus, clams, lobster pappardelle, aglio e olio, steak & french fries. My friends thought they had died and gone to heaven. BEST dinner they had ever ate!

April 2023 — Giovanni made me Pappardelle con il coniglio. It was fantastic. Giovanni's special dishes are made with his heart and I can taste it. He also made fried artichokes that night. Reminded me of ones I ate at a restaurant in Trastevere in Rome.

June 2023 — We were at the restaurant. Giovanni made pasta w/lobster, fried cheese & calamari, cavatelli w/lamb sauce, roast lamb w/potatoes and artichokes and strawberry granita. It was Fabulous!!! This was the meal before Giovanni left for Italy and then Sherre & I met him there.

Aug 2023 — Although it has nothing to do w/ Giovanni cooking; but, traveling in Piedmonte w/ Giovanni & Gianni and having him pick the restaurants & menu, coming to Cetraro and meeting w/his Dad, celebrating Sherre's 70th birthday w/You & Giovanni and his family at the restaurant with the music, dancing & fireworks; and then going on to Capo Vaticano w/ Linda, Giovanni & Francesca. A lifetime memory that you would think could only happen in a dream (and you were right, Capo Vaticano may be the most beautiful place in the world)

Jan 2024 — Celebrating my 70th birthday at Andreoli's. What a meal! Lamb chops, grilled seafood, crudo, and a Very Nice T-shirt from you commemorating my trip to Italy the previous summer.

Nov 2024 — Giovanni made a special dinner for Sherre & I and two other couples, Burrata, spaghetti aglio e olio, grilled calamari, crudo & Bistecca. Everything was cooked perfectly!

In summary, Giovanni has created A LOT of food memories for me, Sherre, Syl & our friends. I didn't mention above but Sherre & I came in one night late and he made us hamburgers and French fries! Fantastic. The overall food memory for me is his passion to serve the best food and the love that he puts into it. He reminds me of my grandfather, my Mom and a couple of her sisters. It's what I call TLC (Tender Loving Care). I can taste TLC and Giovanni puts TLC in to everything he's preparing. You asked about any special dishes. I appreciate so SO much that Giovanni will make special things for me. Rabbit, goat, crudo, fried chicken, hamburgers, granita, tartufo, lamb chops, veal chops, veal Milanese, etc, etc. Also, EVERYONE I have brought there has thoroughly enjoyed their meals.

God granted Sherre & I a gift when Linda, Giovanni and their kids came into our lives. We have so many Great memories that make us smile. THANK YOU and God Bless You all.

Dominic Armato

Within 30 seconds of meeting Giovanni Scorzo, he was waving a massive hunk of cured pork two inches from my nose.

In the early days of Andreoli Italian Grocer—before the dining room expansions, before the Visitation of Saint Fieri, before Phoenix understood the treasure they had right under *their* noses—I would frequently have the place to myself at lunchtime, and I took advantage of that injustice at every possible opportunity. Andreoli was a routine stop for me back when I had the time, two or three lunches a week, usually with the kids in tow, in search of some pasta and whatever regional specialties graced the marker-board that day. And in between perfect renditions of spaghetti alle vongole, gnocchi alla Romana and—God willing—the occasional plate of vitello tonnato, I'd nab a loaf of bread and some items from the case to make another plate of pasta later for dinner.

On one of my early visits, horror of horrors, the pancetta supply had run dry. Sure, I could get pancetta elsewhere, but that meant resigning myself to some kind of sour, factory-quality crap, or worse, the flavorless, prepackaged kibble hanging from a self-service case in a supermarket. I started making alternate dinner plans.

Sensing my anxiety, the young fellow working the counter said he could ask the boss if any of their house-cured pancetta was available, then he quickly turned and disappeared into the kitchen before he could see my eyes pop and my fingers start to twitch.

Moments later, in strode Giovanni, moving briskly and with purpose, holding a curved blade that looked like a holdover from the Italian War of 1551 with one arm and a thick rolled pancetta under the other. He slapped it down on a cutting board, trimmed away the netting, hacked off one end, raised the freshly-cut pancetta to his nose and then stopped dead, pausing to slowly inhale and take in as much of the aroma as his lungs could carry. Grunting his approval, he glanced up, caught me agape, and broke into a sparkling grin.

"Here, smell," he gruffly intoned, jumping around a

worktable and stretching out across the high counter to hold his pancetta at arm's length, close enough for the thick scent of sweet pork and spice with the complex, funky undertones of cured meat to completely wrap itself around my head.

Retracting the pancetta, he bounded back to the cutting board and—now wielding his sword like a scalpel—carefully shaved off a razor-thin, transparent slice for me to sample. And this first taste of Giovanni's house-cured pancetta posed something of a dilemma for me.

It was too good.

I couldn't, in good conscience, render this down for a pasta sauce. It was too delicate, too complex, too deeply imbued with so many subtle characteristics that would be completely obliterated the moment I fried it up in olive oil. I had no idea what I was going to do with it. I just knew I wanted more of it.

"You cure your own pancetta?" I asked, clumsily stating the obvious.

"I make pancetta, salami, soppressata, capicola, culatello . . . the only thing I don't make, I don't make any money," Giovanni replied.

This would not be the last time Giovanni shoved food in my face, and the simplest lesson I have learned from the past fifteen years of visiting Andreoli is that when Giovanni tells you to eat something, you do it.

But it's more than that, and in many ways that first encounter was a distillation of all I have come to love about Giovanni and Andreoli. The food is outstanding, of course, and the once-quiet dining room has evolved the kind of genuine, bustling Third Place that so many restaurants lamely aspire to be. But it's the palpable passion for the craft and the desire—the compulsion—to share it with everyone who walks in the door that makes Giovanni and Andreoli unique. He cares about doing it right. And he wants you to care about doing it right, too. And if you don't understand why that's important, then he will make you understand. Sometimes with joy, sometimes with frustration, often with both. But he will make you understand.

The last time I visited Andreoli, I made the mistake of thinking I could pop in and out in five minutes. It was the peak of the holiday rush, I had one kid awaiting a pickup across town, the other needed some ingredients for a school cooking project, and the moment Giovanni called me over to The King Table, I knew my goose was cooked.

"Dominic! You have to try this. I just got some scallops from Greece. Here, sit down, I'm going to make you something."

"Giovanni, I can't, I have to go get my kid—"

"It will just take a minute, here, sit here, I be right back..."

What could I do?

A few minutes later, he returned with a plate and a pan, and he dished out the most beautiful risotto con capesante it's been my pleasure to slurp down, delicate and soupy, rich with the scent of the scallops' ruddy orange coral, flecked throughout with wisps of bitter melted arugula. But what I loved even more than the dish—and I LOVED the dish—was watching Giovanni flit around the dining room like the patron saint of risotto bestowing blessings upon his guests, pan of scallops and rice in one hand, long wooden spoon in the other, bouncing from person to person, stopping just long enough to offer everybody a spoonful of bliss that was so good he couldn't help but share it with everyone.

Bradley Grauper

One day, I received a call from Giovanni. He's almost whispering.

"Bradley, get 'ovva' here I've—uh got-ah a very much special for you, hurry" or something like that. So I sprint over on my bike. It seemed so urgent. Turns out his friend in Calabria had overnighted—alive mind you— some Jurassic Sea beasts called "*** di ***" which the internet doesn't need to viral kill what's left of the species so let's just asterisk that out. Two massive females each almost the size of a lobster bursting with their eggs, plus two males on a plate, they tasted so INSANE that I went into total tilt and don't remember much of the next fifteen minutes of my life.

It didn't take long for them to be all eaten by some lucky unwitting patrons into whose ears Giovanni whispered, as well as Giovanni's small coterie of friends steadily straggling in one by one, somewhat disheveled, having hurriedly disengaged from whatever they were doing when he had called. Then poof! The pumpkin carriage had disappeared by midnight.

Fast forward ten years later. I'm living in Italy trying to translate lobster at the supermarket with people. There's astiche and arragosta and no one seems to be able to explain the difference (it turned out the English is "cold water lobster" for the one with claws and "warm water lobster" for the one without) except they know the hierarchy of quality: 'shrimp are not as tasty as arragosta which isn't as tasty as astiche which is king. Except, for the almost mythical and impossible to find "sea cicada" of course (a sort of lobster tail come alive which lives its whole life upside down under rocks). It's the tastiest without question. Definitely. Except, of course, the *** di *** but, well, you know, we can't complain if we don't get to enjoy Zeus's wine' or something like that.

Fast forward a few more years. The generous son of a friend wanted to impress me and took me out to the oldest, fanciest, best seafood restaurant in Milan. We must have eaten half of god's underwater creations that night. Just before they brought the wheelbarrow to help me out of the place, my host asked me if I had ever had anything as good as the seafood that night.

After singing high praises for everything we had eaten, I mentioned "this was the best I've ever had since once in Arizona" (which caused everyone to laugh). Then I said, "I know it's crazy, but my friend flew these massive pregnant aliens in alive from Italy called *** di ***.

Just then, the guy walking past dropped his plates without noticing and said, stunned, "you had WHAT? Where?"

It occurred to me that this guy was the owner. Then he said, quite seriously, I have to say, "look, you've eaten a ghost, something that doesn't exist. I've been trying to get them in here for decades and no one who even lives there will admit where they are or who finds them. I can't explain to you how much I want to try and have them here . . ."

Employees are picking up the pieces of broken plates and I don't remember how I weaseled out of that convo without passing on Giovanni's info to that guy. Anyway, off the cuff that's the story and I'm grateful to Giovanni that he was generous with a poor college kid who didn't even yet have a palate by sharing his extraordinary bounty and skills with me over the years!

Many of his dishes come to mind fondly as peerless standards I still hold, but that one especially was so surreal that if it wasn't for the occasional, happenstance recognition by others of that creature's mythical status, I'd probably just conclude I had made it all up in my imagination!

People don't realize what's best about Italy isn't the food, I mean, yes, of course, the food is insane. But it's just the penumbra of the best of Italy, which is the absolutely massive and exaggerated characters who created that food.

Oscar Contesini

There is a piece of Italian theatrical realism in Scottsdale, AZ ... Andreoli where the real Italian lifestyle is staged.

The conduct of this experience is the kitchen ... Around Andreoli's Italian food is consumed not only the most authentic Italian culinary tradition, but a real-life experience made of speeches, meetings, sharing, laughter, feelings and passion ... Andreoli gravitates unique characters from all over the world ready to share their experience at the always reserved table of Giovanni Scorzo, The king of Andreoli ... Yes, Giovanni is the great puppeteer of this comedy that is staged every day, always the same in the canvas but always different in content... The patrons are all unaware actors of this truth theater where the staging slips marked by the three main moments of food tasting: breakfast, lunch, dinner ... In front of a croissant, a coffee, a plate of pasta or a tiramisu, every content is lawful; ranging from politics to sport, from culture to cinema, from art to everyday life, the action takes place in absolute post realism. With Andreoli the concept of reality is overcome: Reality is not staged but the reality that goes on stage

Stephen Rupp

Giovanni, brother-in-law and friend, I am so thankful for the opportunity to experience your wonderful and confident personality. Everything you touch carries your signature—whether it's your food, your laughter, or your way of making people feel welcome and valued. While your culinary talents have certainly made you a beloved figure to everyone who knows you, you are so much more than just a great chef.

My experience with you, Giovanni, has been truly wonderful. From the very beginning, when you married my sister, you made a lasting impression on both me and my wife. I'll never forget when you took the time to travel to Missouri and cook one of your signature dishes for our wedding reception. That night, everyone was talking about your Rigatoni with Sausage & Peas. People couldn't stop asking for the recipe, and it was clear from that moment your cooking has a magic to it.

As I've watched you and my sister build your lives together, I've been fortunate to witness your rise in the business world and all that you've accomplished with your wife, family, and staff. It's been amazing to see the support you've received from everyone around you, and the way you've built something truly special from the ground up and infused everything you touch with your Italian culture. The food, the experience, and having you as my brother-in-law have been some of the most memorable parts of my life.

You've always welcomed me and my family with open arms, and that warmth is something I deeply appreciate. If anyone has ever walked into your restaurant without receiving a hug or an acknowledgment from you, they've truly missed out on one of the most important parts of the experience. Your generosity, love, and connection to people are such a key part of the atmosphere you've created—a perfect reflection of the Italian culture of eating, drinking, and celebrating together.

Over the 30-plus years that I've known you, Giovanni, you've always treated me with kindness and have showered my family and me with countless memorable dinners at your many restaurants. I couldn't even begin to count how many times you've fed us, but every single one of those meals has been a gift. My family loves you and respects your many talents. You can sing, play multiple instruments, and, as you've told me, you even used to be a hairstylist! The sheer number of people you've served over the years is a testament to your dedication to your craft, and I know how much joy it brings you to share such delicious Italian food with everyone who encounters you and your genuine authenticity of your quality of food.

Above all, Giovanni, you have a true love for your family and for Italy. It's always a joy to visit your restaurant and see your family so involved in the business. Together you all have built something beautiful, something that reflects your hard work and commitment to each other. I've always said that my sister is the soul that complements the personality you need to make everything work as one. You two are blessed to have built such a wonderful life, and I'm lucky to be a part of it.

Thank you for all that you've done for me and our family. You've given us so much more than just meals; you've shared your heart and your passion, and for that, I will always be grateful. I look forward to many more years of laughter, good food, and cherished memories.

Finally, I promise I will try to learn more Italian so I can really understand what you and my sister are saying to each other.

Marco Felicoli

I know Giovanni since his restaurant LeccaBaffi. Since then, if I want to eat "real" Italian food, going to Giovanni is the only way to feel at home in Italy. I moved in the US 30 years ago and I always struggling to find a good restaurant, and I man a good restaurant. Andreoli is the place. Giovanni is amazing in the kitchen and with all his guests. Anytime I spoke with him, I understand the passion that he put in all his dishes. All the ingredients are carefully chosen. The fish is all imported fresh from Greece or California, the meat is from Ranch in Montana or Colorado. All the ingredients are good. He imports all the Italian ingredients mostly directly from Italy. There is nothing he cannot do. From pizza, to cornetti, from pasta to soups, from fish to meat and also desserts. His desserts are amazing. Tiramisu' a masterpiece. He even does chocolate tools that my kids love.

The things I love going to Giovanni at Andreoli that is not going to a regular Italian restaurant, but it's an experience. The ambiance is vibrant, and the people are all different. You can also sometime stumble to a celebrity, that can be an actor, a tennis player, and painter or who knows. All the clients enjoy the food because finally they find something that is good and original. Th recipes are the ones that are passed generation by generation with no changes. At Andreoli or you eat what they serve you or you can leave…..in fact if you look at the entrance the sign is pretty explicative.

Stefano Spalvieri

At Giovanni's, it's Italy! We arrived from France in July 2010. What a change of scenery in Arizona, so different from Europe! Quickly, passing on the way to school we discovered an Italian grocery store that we tested and approved for the next 3 years!

Giovanni has won us over with his cuisine, his warm welcome and the Italian atmosphere that reigns in his restaurant! His bread and croissants reminded us of France, the broadcast of football matches was a boon for boys! Our daughter loved spending time with Giovanni, watching him play the piano and sing. I was fascinated by her creative way of cooking. Thanks to him my husband's stay was positive, and they created very strong ties! Since our return to France in 2013, we come back every 2 years to Scottsdale, only for the pleasure of seeing Giovanni and his family again and spending time in this typical Italian restaurant!

Thank you, Giovanni, for all your dishes, pizzas and long discussions! We love you!

John Van Hattem

I have so many good memories from this great man! Wow! Is he gifted with talent. I met Giovanni just by coming to Andreoli's because I loved the food so much. When I met him, we hit it off because my love of great food. He has made so many special things for me. I would bring porterhouse roasts from Colorado, and he would make the best Steak Florentine. My favorite dish he has made me is Veal Bolognese. That is really special and delicious. About a month ago something he did that was so amazing to me. He showed up on a Sunday afternoon at my new house out of the blue and had stopped at the restaurant and made me a huge plate of Pesto pasta. Wow. I had been working all day and was starving. It's almost like he knows what a friend needs. Giovanni you are such a great friend and I'm so blessed to have you as my friend.

Giovanni Martino

I was born in Torino in 1950, lover of the SIMPLE dishes of the true Italian kitchen. My first trip to America was in 1984 to visit family from Torino who'd transferred to Gilroy, California. During my 1986 Gilroy visit, I met Giovanni Scorzo at his Aunt (Elvira) and Uncle's (Giuseppe) pizzeria-Joe's Italian Restaurant. A few years later Giovanni married Linda, a girl from Missouri, who'd transferred to Scottsdale to attend Arizona State University.

In 1988, Giovanni and Linda opened their first restaurant, La Bruschetta, and that was the beginning of a difficult yet rewarding journey, because of Giovanni's desire to succeed in introducing to his American guests, the TRUE and GENUINE Italian cuisine. Every year, I'd visit Giovanni and Linda for 2 or 3 weeks at La Bruschetta or their next restaurant, Babbo Ganzo, in Santa Fe, New Mexico, and the next restaurant, Zingari, San Francisco, to where he landed in Scottsdale, where he opened LeccaBaffi and now his last stop, Andreoli Italian Grocer, known by many.

I personally love simple and genuine dishes that only Giovanni knows how to make. Although simple, my favorite dishes are diverse. For example, Gnocchi al Castelmagno, although diverse, it's simplicity and history is what make it the king of cheeses, there's no other cheese like it in the world. The taste is exceptional, authentic, based in the symbol of good table, and of the good kitchen. If it is aged as it should be, Castelmagno is extraordinary. The aging in the grotto is what gives it it's magic. Unfortunately, the mature aging process has been lost. Castelmagno used to be aged slowly in stables at a high altitude until the cheese formed a rusty layer, where the cheese got softer and the magnificent "veins" came out. Today there is a rush to sell things, and clients ask for white Castelmagno, and let me tell you, they don't know what they are missing. The magic that this cheese has and makes it so unique. There are only a few people left who know the original maturation process and Giovanni is one those people. Giovanni would only order the Castelmagno that had been cured for at least 1 year, even if it was very rare to find.

Another dish that I love is homemade ravioli stuffed with Castelmagno or Ragu (Meat Sauce). It needs to be made by hand, nothing purchased, like the gnocchi all Romana with semolina and pecorino cheese. Even a spaghetti with tomato and parmigiano. For meat dishes, I enjoy a simple Breaded Veal Chop Milanese. What is Milanese? It is a veal Chop, tenderized into a thin medallions, dipped in egg and dressed with bread crumbs. I also really enjoy Giovanni's cakes a lot too, even if their beauty is not like the fancy art dishes presented by famous Italian pastry chefs.

Even in Italy, it is rare to find restaurants dishes that uphold the tradition of holding true to the original simplicity of the dishes. One of my favorite simplest dishes is Riso al Latte (Rice with milk). My mother would make it when I was growing up. It was a 'poor man's' dish, that grandmothers would make once upon a time, but it was delicious. No one makes it anymore. I miss that dish, and knowing that, Giovanni makes it for me when I go to visit him. He prepares it for me the day before, so that I can enjoy it fully the day after. He'd make it so the rice absorbed the milk until it creates a creamy consistency. For me, it's a dish that in some moments, I wouldn't change it for any other dish in the world. When I savor it, the memories of my youth flood my mind. I am so happy and content.

Giovanni Scorzo's cuisine means returning to the original Italian cuisine, including all of the regions. By wisely collecting and not forgetting over the years the precious secrets that his mother and grandmother taught him. Trying Giovanni's cuisine will bring you back to the real genuine tastes, and flavors of once upon a time.

These are the kinds of memories that remind me why I do this. Yes, I love food. Yes, I'm obsessed with ingredients. But at the heart of it all, I love people. And when you walk through the door at Andreoli, you're not just a customer. You're part of the story.

Micheal Giusti

Fortunately, I have had many experiences with food both travelling abroad and at home. Presentation, quality, love, family, treasured stories around the table, aromas and of course taste!

Chef Giovanni Scorzo has created a perfect atmosphere and along with the staff has managed to find and maintain a way of bottling these all together, like a fine Italian wine, every time you walk through the doors at Andreoli's Italian Grocer. His strong Italian heritage, passion and personality are forefront. You get culinary talk, history, politics and thousands of personal and very entertaining stories of life in Calabria. I am honored to have a seat at "The King's Table" to experience life as it is meant to be.

Be it I Peccati Di Gola, Tentazioni, Insalate, the mouthwatering focaccia that melts my wife's heart and dazzles her taste buds. The various and original pasta dishes or the nightly "chefs specials", this Calabrese Italian culinary experience never lets me down. Don't even mention the wood fired pizzas on Tuesday nights (seasonal), the many beverages and the to die for, freshly made cakes and pasticceria.

You get it all. Every time. Every meal. Meticulously presented and watched over by Chef Scorzo.

I love walking in and being greeted like I just belong there. Like I am sitting with my family or around the table with my Zio's or nonno having an espresso and warming my heart.

My wife is now annoyed with me because she is so tired of hearing me say, "honey, that just may be the best meal I have ever had".

Salute Chef Scorzo. Never change! Alla prossima. Ci vediamo . . .

Bob & Judi Johnson

We love Andreoli's, so much so, you can find us there 3 to 5 days a week in recent years. And if that sounds excessive, know that we aren't the only ones. Giovanni has done so much more than just create a place for great food. He has created an amazing community here in Scottsdale. We've met people and made friends we otherwise would have had no opportunity to ever meet, while bonding over the most incredible dishes. His playful teasing and mischievous grin starts when we walk in. He lets us know we owe him rent because we are there so much. But know, if Giovanni starts to tease you, know you have made it to family status.... And when you get to family status, you get access to a taste of creations that aren't on the menu. Everything on the menu is exceptional. But when Giovanni says, oh, I just made this or that, I'll bring you a taste, my excitement hits the roof immediately. Whether it's freshly cured pancetta, or a biancaneve sandwich, or an anchovy pasta sauce, you can't believe the flavors in the food. The dishes are clean and simple, but the tastes wake up your palate and transport you to Italy. This is not a chain restaurant with cookie-cutter spaghetti and meatballs. This is real Italian cuisine that runs the gamut of ingredients, so you never feel like you're having the same food on repeat. And if that weren't enough, you get Giovanni's cheeky stories.... almost always obnoxious and inappropriate, but always hysterical and harmless. This restaurant has done more than fill our stomachs. It has given my family core memories and friendship we will treasure forever.

Recipes

Pasta
(Fettuccine, Taglierini, Lasagne, Tagliatelle, Pappardelle) . 11

Spaghetti al Pomodoro di Nonna Sofia
(Spaghetti with Tomato Sauce) 22

Minestra di Fava
(Fava Bean Soup). 33

Costata di Vitello alla Milanese
(Milanese-style Veal Chop) 41

Sogliola alla Mugnaia
(Filet of Sole with Lemon and Butter) 47

Impepatina di Cozze
(Italian Peppered Mussels) 50

Pitticelli i Milangiani
(Eggplant Fritters). 57

Bistecca Fiorentina
(Florentine Steak) 101

Sugo di Carne
(Meat Sauce). 131

Bollito di Manzo
(Boiled Beef). 135

Salsa Verde
(Green Sauce). 137

Rigatoni alla Amatriciana
(Rigatoni with Guanciale, Tomato and Pecorino) 150

Pappardelle con Costine di Maiale
(Pappardelle with Pork Short Ribs) 156

Chronology

Here's a chronology of key events in my life, including my childhood, my training as a chef, marrying Linda and the birth of our three children, Francesca, Gian Paul, Angelino, as well as the restaurants I've worked at or founded.

- I'm born in Calabria, the child of Mamma Adele and Serafino.
- The family moves from Calabria, in the south of Italy, to Liguria, in northern Italy.
- I attend culinary school and work in a variety of restaurants in Italy.
- Gianni is short for Giovanni, a nickname.
- After meeting Linda in Firenze, I moved to the United States and we got married.
- I open my first restaurant, La Bruschetta, which I co-run with Linda.
- Our first child, Francesca Rose, is born.
- We open and run our second restaurant, Babbo Ganzo in Santa Fe, New Mexico.
- Our first son, Giovanni Paul (Gian Paul), is born.
- We open and run our third restaurant, Zingari in San Francisco, California.
- Our second son, Piero Angelo (Angelino), is born.
- We open and run our fourth restaurant, *LeccaBaffi*,

in Scottsdale, Arizona. During the same time, we opened our fifth establishment, Galileo Bakery.

- 2007 - Andreoli opens in Scottsdale, Arizona.
- April 2022 - I am nominated for James Beard Award for Best Chef in the Southwest
- 2024 - I decide it is time to put together my recollections, my philosophy about cooking and food, as well as to share some key recipes into a book. I decide to call it *Shut Up and Eat*.
- 2025 – *Shut Up and Eat* is published.

About the Author

Photo Credit: Brian Goddard Photography

Giovanni Scorzo was born in the Calabria region in southwest Italy and raised in Liguria, which is also known as the Italian riviera, on the northwest coast of the Mediterranean. He first learned how to cook from his mother and perfected his skills in culinary school and later in several different fine restaurants throughout Italy, including the Five Star Savoy restaurant in Florence.

As chef and owner of Andreoli Italian Grocer in Scottsdale, Arizona, Scorzo was a Best Chef in the Southwest finalist in the 2022 James Beard Foundation Awards, which are considered the Oscars of the culinary world. He has appeared numerous times on the popular

Food Channel program hosted by Guy Fieri, *Diners, Drive-ins and Dives*.

According to the Andreoli website, "Chef Scorzo is the creator of a piece of theatrical realism, Andreoli where real Italian lifestyle is staged. Italian food is consumed not only by the most authentic culinary tradition, but a real-life experience made of speeches, meetings, sharing, laughter, feeling and passion.

"Giovanni is Andreoli's great puppeteer, showcasing his culinary prowess and larger-than-life personality. A meal at Andreoli is staged daily, always the same on the canvas but different in content. The patrons are all unaware actors of this truth theater where the staging slips marked by the three central moments of food tasting: breakfast, lunch, and dinner."

"With Andreoli, the concept of reality is overcome. Reality is not staged but a reality that goes on stage."